GIG FOR LIFE

GIG
FOR
LIFE

The ultimate no bulls#♪t
guide for musicians

Georges Elchakieh

scarlip

GIG FOR LIFE
The Ultimate No Bullshit Guide for Musicians

ISBN	978-1-5445-3692-7	*Hardcover*
	978-1-5445-3693-4	*Paperback*
	978-1-5445-3694-1	*Ebook*
	978-1-5445-3475-6	*Audiobook*

For Chuck

CONTENTS

ENCORE

INTRODUCTION

Let me tell you a story about two musicians. Both worked at Walmart and dreamed of making money playing music. The first one, let's call him Midnight Dave, was extremely talented in every way: the abs, the look, the wardrobe, the magical fingers. Girls were all over him. But Midnight Dave was a flake. He had a bad attitude and pissed people off because he thought he was the end-all of the music world and his break was just around the corner.

Still, Midnight Dave kept getting gigs. One band would drop him and another would hire him because his talent was that special. He had the world at his fingertips.

Time passed. Midnight Dave grew older. He got himself a beer belly, and his hair started falling out. He continued burning bridges, only now he was making enemies with the club owners as well as with musicians. Even if a band hired him, the joints refused to let him play because he had such a bad reputation, so it became harder to make money from his talent. His girlfriend had popped out two of his kids, but Midnight Dave never had the balls to put a ring on her finger and marry her, or at least commit to sticking around.

Midnight Dave kept getting the typical wedding and corporate gigs, and he still did the same stupid shit. He showed up late, didn't learn his tunes, disrespected the audience, and took his band and employers for granted. Only now, he was overweight and bald on top of it all, and no one wanted to hire him because there were younger guys with hipper dance moves and more commitment. As a result, he only worked once or twice a week. Money started getting thin, so he began selling his soul—taking the gigs he once refused because he thought they were beneath him. In the end, Midnight Dave had to haul ass back to Walmart as a resentful, overweight, middle-aged has-been.

The second musician, let's call him Pro Joe, had half the talent Midnight Dave did, but he built a stable career playing and teaching music. He had a wonderful family, bought a nice house, and made successful investments. Whereas Midnight Dave ended up back at Walmart, Pro Joe made money from his music into late-middle age, and it was all because of one fixable difference—attitude. Pro Joe learned to say, "May I please," "If you don't mind," "Sure, why not," "How can I help," and "Thank you for the opportunity." He didn't see himself as God's gift to the universe. He prioritized rehearsals. He respected the stage, his bandmates, and the club owners who provided it. He appreciated and connected with the fans who showed up at his gigs. Pro Joe treated every night like a Saturday night and gave 100 percent to each performance.

There's nothing wrong with Walmart, but if you aspire to a life as a musician, you have to do what is necessary to get there. No one has the young body, long hair, and sexy moves forever. And only 0.1 percent, if that, of all musicians reach the fame of a Beyoncé or Justin Timberlake. Hasn't *American Idol* proven that it takes more than incredible talent to play to stadiums full of adoring fans?

For the rest of us, a successful career in music will involve playing in bars, clubs, hotels, corporate gigs, cruise ships, and wedding venues. That career can be just as fulfilling and meaningful—if you're willing to be like Pro Joe and work at the fundamentals.

This book is for the rest of us.

"I JUST WANT TO PLAY, MAN"

Many musicians join or start a band with one goal in mind: "I just want to play, man." They are consumed with practicing their instrument five or six hours a day. Why not do the same with people who have the same goal?

Very soon, however, they find out it's not that simple.

If you've tried to put a band together, the following might sound familiar: You find a drummer, guitarist, keyboard player, and singer, and everyone commits to rehearsals three days a week. You book a gig at a local nightclub, and everyone agrees to the stated pay. But then the keyboard player stops showing up to rehearsals, and the singer turns out to be a crazy prima donna with a beautiful voice who refuses to learn her parts. After you play the gig at the joint, the guitarist argues that he should be paid more, even though he agreed to the amount beforehand. Another band offers your drummer more money, and he leaves without a second thought. You find another drummer, but he's a "Midnight Dave" who has an affair with the club owner's wife, and you get banned from playing there.

This list is only a short list of the stress that can come your way if you start a band or join one. It can be overwhelming, and I've known many musicians who run into these problems, become discouraged, and give up before they really get started. I've also known musicians who sabotage their own dreams by being the drama-causing singer or Casanova Midnight Dave.

My goal is to prevent both scenarios from happening to you.

WORK THE SYSTEM

No matter where you are in your music career, this book can help. I have developed a system for every aspect of creating and running a successful business as a band—and yes, it is a business, and you must treat it as such. This system involves tips for the following:

- Hiring musicians
- Organizing a repertoire
- Planning rehearsals
- Building relationships with bandmates and club owners
- Booking gigs
- Preparing for gigs
- Mastering onstage behavior and wardrobe
- Interacting with the audience
- Building, refining, and systematizing your business
- Preparing for unexpected disruptions

I even provide a system for capturing your system—that is, writing down what you've done, so you can replicate it over and over with different bands, club owners, and audiences, enabling you to enjoy an exciting lifelong career playing music.

No matter what kind of band you form or what gigs you play, you will always deal with four interpersonal elements in this business: yourself, your bandmates, your partners (venue owners, manager, and staff), and your audience. The chapters, or "tracks," in this book fall into four sets that cover these four elements—from figuring out your vision and deciding what kind of music you want to play (Set List 1), to finding the right bandmates and building those relationships (Set List 2), to working with club owners professionally and respectfully (Set List 3), to building a community with your audience (Set List 4). When you finish the sets, you'll enjoy an encore, where you'll learn how to refine and systematize the business you've created and how to prepare for worst-case scenarios before they happen.

In the pages that follow, you'll find diagrams and spreadsheets, as well as real-life stories that illustrate how this system works and why you need it. You'll find lessons that go beyond your life in a band, tips that will make you a better husband or wife, son or daughter, father or mother, brother or sister, leader, entertainer, customer—in short, they'll make you a better person. I don't believe in work–life balance because I don't believe you can separate you from you. Everywhere you go, you are all that you are. You're not the entertainer outside the house and husband or wife inside. It's *all* you.

During my first meeting with my drum teacher when I was seventeen, he said, "It's impossible to be a great drummer without first changing your very core. I don't give a shit if you ever play the drums, but through the drums, your life will change." He was right. Inspired by this teacher's life lessons, I developed my own philosophy over the years, systematized it, and created this book as a result. Whether you get a gig a week or one a year, if you apply the lessons shared here, you will change on the inside, which is even more important than playing in a club every night for the rest of your life. The one requirement is that you learn how to work the system—and then do it, always allowing yourself to be coachable along the way.

Success is not in the knowing, but in the doing. If you work the system as suggested here, you will avoid much of the stress and disappointment just described, and you'll rediscover the joy of music that has perhaps gotten buried under the obstacles and frustration.

FROM ONE BAND TO HUNDREDS

How do I know this system works? I've been working it, accidentally and intentionally, for over thirty-five years. This system for hiring, rehearsing, behaving, and building relationships has allowed me to create and book bands who make a living off of playing their music.

My love of music started when I was seven or eight. My five siblings and I shared one bedroom, so there were nights when my bed was the living room couch. I remember lying there one night, listening to the song "Bésame Mucho," so annoyed that my brother's friend was talking to me and I couldn't really listen to the song. A few years later I saw *Saturday Night Fever*, and that was it: I wanted to be John Travolta. I was fascinated by pop music of that time, and I listened to the songs over and over to hear how the instruments and words all came together.

Shortly after I moved to Ottawa, Canada, at age fourteen, I started music lessons for the first time. I had planned on taking guitar like my oldest brother Nick, but the school didn't offer guitar lessons. One day I was working in Nick's restaurant, and I told the cook that they didn't offer guitar.

"Fuck guitar," Richard said. "Take the drums. I play drums." Richard was cool. He had long hair and a cute girlfriend. Why wouldn't I want to be like Richard? So I took drums, and my brother Tony bought me my first set.

A few years later, I started taking one-on-one lessons with Chuck Burrows, and my life changed forever. Chuck didn't just teach me music; he taught me about life, and much of the philosophical component of this book comes from those lessons.

In the fall of 1987, I moved to Montreal to study music at Concordia University...and I quickly learned that the classroom wasn't for me. I wanted to get out there and play. Through word of mouth and sheer relentlessness, I formed a band, and by February, we were the most-booked group in the city.

After throwing a huge drummer's party shortly after, I suddenly became a well-known musician in Montreal. Every drummer belongs to a band, and because I had met most of the city's drummers at my party, I had access to hundreds of musicians, as well as the clubs where they play, so my band stayed very busy.

Soon, however, because of the issues mentioned earlier and more, I found that leading the band was too stressful, and I decided to work for another group.

Around the same time, I helped my best friend put a band together with my girlfriend as the lead singer. Then I started booking gigs on their behalf, tapping into the relationships I had formed with club owners over the previous years. This was the first time I started putting my system into action, though at the time, I didn't see it that way. I was just a friend helping a friend.

Over the next few years, I started three more bands of my own, including Elchakieh, which became the talk of the town. In 1997, at the invitation of a Hong Kong agency, we moved to Jakarta, Indonesia, and started gigging all over Asia.

All along this journey, I read a lot of books on management, investment, real estate, personal improvement, and more. In 1999, I read *The Winner Within* by former Lakers' head coach Pat Riley, in which he lays out his coaching method. Then I started applying his techniques to the way I led my band, and it worked. I also realized that over the previous twelve years, I had been following my own method for forming and booking bands, though I had not formalized the system or even thought of it as one.

The same year that I read Riley's book, I saw Cirque du Soleil in Hong Kong. As I watched, my brain buzzed with possibilities. They were able to create the same beautiful vibe across seven massive cirques that performed simultaneously around the world. Could I do the same thing with bands?

Over the next few years, this idea bounced around in my brain. At that point I was thirty-five years old, unmarried, moving from country to country every four months, living out of hotels all across Asia. But I was growing tired of that life. Then I got married and had a son, and I really wanted to figure out a way to stay in one place while organizing and sending out bands all over Asia.

So in 2003, I tried out my idea. I let someone else take over the band I had formed and sent them off to Indonesia and then China, while I stayed in Thailand and started another band. Both bands failed. I hadn't given clear guidelines to the person leading my band, I hired the wrong people for the second band, and I put the plan in play too quickly. I didn't understand culture back then, and the guys I brought in didn't share my vision and values. So I brought my first band back, got rid of the new guys who didn't fit, and rejoined my friends Mike and Marc as their front man. Over the next four years, we continued gigging while I kept refining my system.

Soon, however, reality set in, and I realized I needed a better plan to feed my family. Using my music background and the experience I had gained teaching drums for seven years when I was still living in Montreal, I spent a year and a half designing a chain of music schools with Marc.

In late 2007 I was set to move back to Canada to put this music school plan in place, but after a conversation with some friends weeks before we left, I changed my mind.

"Fuck that," I told my wife, Julie, one night. "I'm going to use this chain model with bands." I launched el-live Productions the very next day, and since then we have been actively employing this system of starting and booking bands.

Over the last fourteen years, we have had the honor of working with hundreds of artists, young and old. They have allowed us to coach them using the lessons learned from my own mistakes and successes. We have hired every musician. We have created each band's look, feel, dress, and repertoire. We have coached them in how to best conduct themselves on and offstage.

Many came in frustrated and disappointed with their music careers, but as they worked the system, they became confident, professional people, who looked at life with excitement and played music at the same time. Many of them own homes, have families, enjoy successful investments, and daily live out their dream of having a gig for life.

COUNT IT OFF

If you want to be the next Top Forty superstar, this book is not for you. I wish you the best of luck, but you might as well put this book down and start pursuing your dream.

However, if you want to enjoy playing music for the rest of your life, whether full-time or part-time—and no matter where you currently are on the journey—this book is for you. More than that, this book is a necessity.

We'll start this journey with you: what do *you* want?

ME

VISION

n the mid-1980s, Ottawa, Canada, was pretty conser-
vative, and the options for an aspiring musician like
me were limited. Montreal, on the other hand, had a
thriving music scene, so I decided that was where I
needed to be.

I applied to Concordia University, which only accepted
four drummers each year. My music teacher, Chuck
Burrows, spent a year and a half preparing me for the
audition. Chuck said, "Look, they are not going to teach
you anything I haven't taught you. Here I can give you the
knowledge, but I cannot give you the environment. At
university you will be surrounded by many musicians
who are at least as good as you are, or much better, and in
Montreal, there will be many live music clubs you can go

to and maybe play some gigs. You can practice till you're blue in the face, but nothing beats the real-life experience of being onstage and dealing with musicians, bar managers, and audiences."

Chuck put a huge dose of fear in me, then he ran me through the wringer, practicing every style of music, from bossa nova to rock to basic jazz, and improving my reading just so I could get through the audition.

When the day finally came, I was nervous as hell. There must have been thirty-five to forty drummers in the waiting room. We could hear musicians auditioning all over the halls. When I heard the other drummers playing I thought, *Holy shit. These guys are smoking!*

Finally, it was my turn. I walked in to find four judges and teachers sitting behind a table, and a drum set sitting across the room. Someone handed me a sheet of music I'd never seen and told me to play. Then they gave me another sheet and another. For what seemed like a billion minutes, but was more like fifteen, I played everything—R & B, bossa nova, samba, funk, rock, and some drum rudiments. It was really a test of fundamentals: Can you sight read? Can you play syncopated notes? Are you familiar with all the styles? The point was to find out if I knew the basics that would carry me through their program.

That audition was one of the most nerve-racking experiences I've ever gone through. Three to four months later, I received an envelope from Concordia. I opened it with shaking hands and pulled out the sheet of paper. The first line started, "We are pleased to inform you..." I couldn't believe it.

Even though I worked hard at playing the drums, I had major imposter syndrome and frequently thought, *Who am I to play music? I'm sure everybody's better than me.* This acceptance letter told me I was doing what I was supposed to do. It was the validation I needed to keep going.

From the moment I got off the bus in Montreal, I felt like I was on a different planet. People dressed differently, talked differently, and walked differently than they did in Ottawa. Girls had blue hair and wore boots. Guys had long hair and wore earrings. They all looked hip and artistic, completely at ease with who they were. I heard Italian, French, Greek, and other languages spoken all around me. The city had such a vibrant energy. I was in heaven.

From those first days in Montreal, I was focused on one thing: starting a band and playing music. I just wanted to play James Brown and Aretha Franklin with other musicians who loved that genre as much as I did. That was the whole reason I had left Ottawa to study at Concordia. That was the whole reason I was taking a theory class. Soon, I got tired of waiting. If the whole reason I was going to university was to be in a band, why not just be in a band?

By November 1987, I had assembled my first band, According to Roger, and by February 1988, we were booked twenty-six out of twenty-eight days in a city where most bands were booked Friday and Saturday each week, if they were lucky. Seven years later, I started my second real band, Elchakieh, and I've never looked back. But it all started because I knew what I wanted.

The journey to a successful music career begins with you. You have to know what you want, where you want to play, who you want to play with. Only then can you take the first step in the right direction.

SELF-ASSESSMENT

Songs come and go. Bars come and go. The musicians you play with come and go. What remains is you—who you are and what you are all about. The greatest song you will ever write is the song of your life, and that tune will come through your music.

One disclaimer: when you do a self-assessment, you shouldn't suddenly discover that you don't actually know how to play the guitar or drums or whatever you want to play. We're starting with the assumption that you can play.

With that out of the way, let's start by figuring out who you are, where you want to go, and what's in your way.

Who Are You?

When I came from Lebanon, all I really knew about music was that I loved it. I didn't know that music had categories or styles. I didn't know what R & B was or what any labels were. I was all passion and no knowledge.

One day when I was still living in Ottawa, my music teacher played Ike and Tina Turner for me. I started jumping up and down. "That's it!" I shouted. "That's the music. That's the sound I want to play!" I didn't know who it was, but that was what I had been wanting.

"Okay," Chuck said. "This is Ike and Tina Turner. It's R&B."

When he played another song, he told me it was Elvis Presley. He saw my blank stare and changed tactics. "Okay, it's like the Beatles. You know the Beatles?"

"I don't know, man," I said.

Chuck looked so bummed out. I could almost read his thoughts: *How am I going to teach this kid?*

But Chuck was a wonderful person. He asked me to bring him a box of blank TDK D90 cassette tapes, and every time he taught me a new groove, he spent hours recording compilations of all of the bands in that genre. He loved big jazz bands, so he would fill those cassettes up with Dizzy Gillespie, Buddy Rich, and Duke Ellington. After he taught me R & B, he gave me ninety minutes of James Brown, Marvin Gaye, Stevie Wonder, and Aretha Franklin. He did the same for rock, funk, fusion, and the music label ECM with musicians like Pat Matheney, Keith Jarrett, and Jack DeJohnette. Even though I ended up playing mostly R & B in my career, Chuck took the time to explain *all* the musical styles, which most musicians don't bother with.

My hunger and respect for R&B in particular was insatiable. I learned the history of jazz and funk. I studied the history of drums, and after hearing James Brown, I looked up all of his drummers. There wasn't a book on the genre that I didn't devour.

I didn't know any of the greats' names, but when I heard that tune by Ike and Tina Turner and then James Brown, I knew that was the music I wanted to play. For me, the answer to "Who are you?" became "I am a drummer who plays R & B in the busiest band in town."

Maybe you don't like R&B. Maybe you want to play in a blues band, wear T-shirts and jeans onstage, and play your harmonica. Maybe you dream of playing in country and western bars until you're eighty. That's cool too. The important thing is to figure out who *you* are and what kind of music excites *you*.

Knowing what kind of music you like is only one part of figuring out who you are. You also need to think about other aspects of your very nature:

- What kind of people do you like to hang out with?
- What kind of people rub you the wrong way?
- Are you outgoing or introverted? Do you get energized by people or do crowds make you want to escape to your own place?
- Are you confrontational, or do you hate arguments?
- Do things always have to go your way?
- Do you hate taking orders?
- Are you lazy or ambitious?

- Are you organized or fly-by-the-seat-of-your-pants?
- Do you go out of your way to help people, or do you keep to yourself?
- Are you loud or soft-spoken?
- Do loud people get on your nerves?
- Are you bugged by overly calm people?
- Are you flexible, or do last-minute changes drive you crazy?
- Do you like to travel, or do you hate sleeping in hotels?
- Do you keep your word no matter what? Do you expect others to do the same?

In addition, take time to think about your strengths. I know that I am not the most disciplined person in the world. I'm not the kind who gets up to run at 6:00 a.m. But when I start a project, I will not slow down until it's done. I'm also an excellent negotiator, I'm persuasive, and I know how to inspire musicians to be the best they can be.

By focusing on my strengths, and not my weaknesses, I have been able to connect the dots and use my unique combination of talents to build bands and then a business. You can do the same. Yes, it's good to be aware of your weaknesses, but spend your energy really understanding and building your strengths rather than trying to fix your weaknesses. You can always hire people to fill in those gaps.

You are going to be connecting yourself with a group of people, so you better figure out who you are first, so you know who you work best with.

WHERE DO YOU WANT TO GO?

In your mind, there's likely a movie playing that goes something like this: "I want to be in a rock band, become super big, and stay together forever like the Stones." Or "I want to play in a cafe with my acoustic guitar" or "I want to play in a high-energy party band in packed night clubs" or "I just want to sing jazz classics with a piano player."

Every musician has a vision of what their band looks like. Before you can take the first step to produce that movie, you have to figure out exactly what's playing in your head:

- What kind of music will you play?
- How often do you want to play? Several nights a week? Or one weekend a month?
- Do you want to be a full-time musician or keep a day job? Do you want to live off your music, or is this just for fun?
- How many people do you want in your band? Do they need to have experience in your genre? How many years' experience? Do they want them to play part-time or full-time?
- Where will you find these musicians?
- What kind of venue do you want to play in?

Nightclubs? Bars? Weddings?

- Where will you find these gigs?
- What kind of audience comes to your gigs? What do the ladies wear? What do the gents wear? Are they coming straight from work or dressing up first?
- How far are you willing to travel?
- How many rehearsals will you do a week?
- How much of the organization will you do yourself?
- How much money are you expecting?

There isn't a right or wrong answer to any of these questions. You simply have to figure out what is in *your* movie. Then you can take it out of your head and write it down.

THE ONE THING

In case you haven't already figured this out, let me break it to you: decision making is hard. But it's something you'll have to do throughout your life and music career, so why not have a system for it?

My system involves asking myself, "What is the one thing…" whenever I am faced with a decision. For example:

- What is the one thing that makes me want to join this band? Is it travel, the quality of musicians, the style of music?

- What is the one reason I want to sing this song?
- What is one thing I want to get out of this negotiation about X?
- What is the thing I can do in this situation that makes everything else easier or unnecessary?

If you keep the one thing in mind, you can ignore the other annoyances, make a decision, and move on.

What's in Your Way?

Now that you know what you want, you need to look at what might stand in the way of achieving those dreams. What obstacles might come up inside your own head or in your lifestyle, habits, and personality? It's better to be aware of those obstacles up front, so you can proactively address them. If you don't, no one else will because the hard truth is, no one else really cares about what you're trying to do. It's up to you to figure out what's in your way so you don't sabotage your dreams before you get started.

For example, I've worked with many talented musicians who have no control over their sleep habits. Some don't go to bed until ten in the morning and then wake up late in the afternoon. As a result, they are often run-down and sick, and that affects their ability to perform. More than that, it affects their whole life and can single-handedly prevent them from achieving anything.

Another common obstacle is a boyfriend or girlfriend. You've probably heard stories about the could-have-been hockey player who didn't move to Boston because his girlfriend didn't agree, then three weeks later they broke up, so the player lost the girl *and* his opportunity to play in the NHL.

You may need to have some tough conversations with your significant other up front. Is your partner the jealous type? That could be a problem if you're out late every night playing gigs that are filled with attractive young fans. Is your partner insecure? That could be a problem if you're the lead singer and fans are constantly hitting on you.

Many musicians have day jobs, especially when they are first starting out. As they discover, conflicts arise: if you have rehearsal on Wednesdays at noon, what do you do? You might be tempted to say, "The hell with it. I'll quit my job." But then how do you pay the rent?

You cannot walk blindly into your musical career. You have to consider the potential obstacles up front and figure out how you're going to handle them. Here are some areas to consider as part of your self-assessment.

- **Habits**: What time do you go to bed every night? What time do you wake up? Do you have an alcohol or drug problem? It will likely get worse once you're on the road and both are readily available. Are you willing to limit or give up drinking for your career?

- **Relationships**: Do you have a significant other? Are they okay with you coming home at four in the morning every night? Are they okay with you driving around with the boys in the band? Do you have kids? How much downtime do you need to set aside to spend with them?

- **Commitments**: Do you have a day job? How will you fit in rehearsals and gigs and still keep your job? If you quit your day job, how many paid gigs will you need to have to cover your monthly costs?

- **Headspace**: Are you focused and dedicated to doing whatever you need to do? Are you willing to put in four thousand hours of rehearsal to enjoy those forty minutes of glory onstage? Are you ready for the thrilling but unforgiving emotional rollercoaster that lies ahead?

- **Personal weaknesses**: Are you lazy? Do you get easily offended? Are you rude and disrespectful? Do you have anger issues? None of those qualities will serve you well in this business. You're going to get judged harshly for your hair and clothing. People will criticize your songs. To create the career you want, you will need the help of club owners and fans, and no one wants to work with a bonehead. Remember the story of Midnight Dave.

- **Musical skills**: A pep talk only goes so far when it comes to musical skills. There are limitations to bullshit. If your skill is three chords, go ahead and play for your mom, but know that you're going to have to greatly up your abilities before you can play in a nightclub. Don't let that stop you from starting, but be realistic about where you are, and find people who are willing to play with you as you grow. Then work on your skills to get to where you really want to be.

MORE SKILLS MEANS
MORE OPPORTUNITIES

Every week, our band According to Roger had to pay $250 for the sound system we used. In those days, that was a lot of money. I did the math in my head and decided to buy a sound system. I called the Bank of Nick, my brother, and he sent me $14,000 for a brand-spanking-new system.

Only one problem: I didn't know how to turn it on. So I connected with my ecosystem, specifically my friend Mark Ewanchyna, who gave me a crash course in how to use it. I also did the same thing I did when I learned French and English, when I gathered the band, when I booked my first gig: I asked questions, a lot of questions.

Next thing you know, I started getting calls: "Hey, Georges, I hear you know how to work a sound system." People started paying *me* $250 to work a sound system, instead of the other way around. I started doing sound for the biggest stars in the Middle East.

Long before I began doing sound, I started teaching drums to make a little money on the side, and it became a complete business by itself. So now, I was making a living from three different revenue streams: teaching drums, working my sound system, and gigging.

These skills not only put money in my pocket; they also increased my value as a musician, which helped my overall career, especially when I founded my company twenty-five years later.

Yes, you need to assess and polish your musical skills. But the more skills you have outside the ability to play your instrument, the more you will make yourself stand out in the crowd. Unless you're the best of the best—and very few of us are—you should think about adding to your skills suitcase. If you're a musician, learn how to sing, and if you are a singer, learn how to play an instrument.

This alone will add 50 percent more gigs to your schedule. Adding skills is the best way to increase your insurance policy for gigging for life.

Yes, I know you *just want to play, man.* But do yourself a favor and start considering these questions now. Take a good long look in the mirror and be honest with yourself. Start identifying and dealing with your demons today. In doing so, you will minimize stress and maximize joy in this journey.

Here's my ultimate advice in the area of overcoming obstacles, especially those caused by your own internal emotional, mental, and personality issues: take ownership of your life. Admit when something is your fault. It may sound unreasonable to blame yourself for some things, but it's actually freeing because if it's your fault, you can fix it. If you blame someone else or fate or circumstances beyond your control, how the hell do you fix that?

YOU ARE PART OF AN ECOSYSTEM

As you self-assess and start working on the areas that need fixing—in other words, as you center yourself, your emotions, your mental state, your skills—you also center the other parts of your ecosystem: your band, your venues, and your fans.

That said, you shouldn't wait to start or join a band until you are perfectly centered, because that will never happen. Start where you are, find others to join you, and then keep working on you.

Your band, whether started by you or someone else, is a structure that houses individuals to share your dreams. That group of similarly imperfect people then moves into an actual physical structure—a venue with owners and risk-takers on your behalf—which will lead you to play for an audience, at least some of whom will inevitably become part of your fan base. This ecosystem is an ever-present, vital part of your experience as a musician—a system of four circles working together, always rolling forward and upward. Those circles never stop because we never arrive at perfection. There is always more to learn, so enjoy the journey.

The thing about these circles is that you don't have control over most of them, even if you manage your band like a dictator. The only one you can control is *you*: how much you practice, how you interact with your bandmates, how you form relationships with the venue managers, and how you present yourself to your audience.

So take the time to self-assess. Take the time to figure out who you are, where you're going, and what's in your way. If you take the time to center yourself from the beginning, the rest of the ecosystem will follow.

THE RIGHT ENVIRONMENT

I cannot emphasize enough the importance of having the right environment. I would not have accomplished what I have without the right ecosystem around me. Chuck's lessons, Chuck pushing me to go to Concordia, the amazing musicians I met at the university—all of these "circles" provided what I needed to succeed. The same is true for you.

FIX AND GO

Okay, now you have thought about who you are and what you want to do. You know there are pitfalls and obstacles. You will need to be honest with yourself and make some changes. Choosing this path might cost you a day job or losing a girlfriend or boyfriend who doesn't understand. You will lose sleep. You will be faced with your insecurities and personal weaknesses. Knowing all that, do you still want to do this?

If so, let's go. Don't wait until you have it all figured out. Just fix what you know and keep going. The next track will help you figure out where to start.

CHALLENGE

DO A GIG, ANY GIG

Whoever you are right now, wherever you are right now, you have to get started. Go out and do a gig today, even if it's just for your aunt Edna. If the theme at the heart of your answers to the self-assessment is "I want to play music," then you have to pick up an instrument and play. You have to get started, even if you don't have all the details worked out.

Share where you're gigging, and tag me with #vision #gigforlife.

WHAT'S NEXT?

Soon after he moved to Canada, my oldest brother Nick bought a pizzeria, and like typical immigrants, we all worked there—my mom, dad, four brothers, and two sisters-in-law. At 4:00 p.m. every day, the same thing happened: people started calling to place orders. At 3:55, nothing. At 4:00, all three phones started ringing like crazy.

My older brother Joseph and I worked the early evening shifts, which we called first supper, to help with the rush. We attended different schools, so we each had to take several buses to get to the pizzeria, and we didn't speak much English or French. We knew that our family was counting on us, and we knew if we missed any of those buses, we'd be late, and missing the dinner rush would be devastating for business. By the time we arrived, we were already stressed, and then we had to run to the back, put on our aprons, and start making pizzas because those yellow order slips already lined the entire counter.

One day, my oldest brother Nick could see the anxiety on Joseph's face as he frantically tried to keep up with the orders. Finally, Nick walked over and stacked all of the yellow slips on one side of the counter. Then he took the top slip and laid it on the counter in front of my brother and said, "Joseph, one pizza at a time."

Joseph took a deep breath, rolled out the dough, dressed the pizza, put it in the oven, and moved the first slip to the other side. Done. Then he took the next slip, rolled out the dough, dressed the pizza, put it in the oven, and moved the next slip, and so on and so on. The mountain of slips still sat on the counter, but he only looked at one at a time.

Now, imagine he focused *only* on the one yellow slip in front of him, without any awareness of the mountain of slips ahead. He might have become discouraged for a different reason: thinking that he was working on his last pizza only to find out there was another and another and another. It would have been tough to keep going. But because he saw the "peak" first, he knew that there was a mountain to climb. He knew what he was up against from the beginning.

Once you figure out what you want out of your career in music, you may feel as overwhelmed as Joseph did. You may ask yourself, "How do I put a proper band together? Who will want to perform with me? Where will I find top-notch musicians? Where and how will I find and book gigs?" All of these questions and more will crowd your mind. When that happens, pause and remember Nick's advice: one pizza at a time. Keep the peak at the forefront of your mind, and then take that first step.

In this track, we'll talk about where to start and how to keep moving forward.

DREAM BIG, THINK SMALL

Now that you know who you are and what you want to do—in other words, now that you see the peak—it's time to start climbing. This track will not tell you the exact steps to take because there are a million ways to get to where you want to go. My goal is to help you think through what needs to be done, so you can figure out what *you* need to do, one step at a time.

The key is to think small, very small. For example, "start a band" is not a single step. It's a project made up of many smaller tasks such as "find a local nightclub that hires top 40 bands." "Go listen to the band." "Talk to the lead guitarist." One step at a time means one call, one message, one visit—literally, one step at a time. You can and will figure out the rest later.

Your two biggest projects right now are probably finding an existing band to play with or putting a band together, and finding places to perform. In both cases your very first step is probably a phone call. Who do you know who plays the kind of music that you want to play? Who do you know who knows someone who plays the kind of music you want to play? Do you know which nightclubs feature live music that perform your kind of music? Do you know which nights feature live bands?

Beyond a phone call, your next step might be any of these:

- Drive to a bar where you'd like to play, have a beer, and listen to the band
- Write an Instagram message to a bass player you knew in high school
- Draft a post on a local musician Facebook group (or your preferred social media platform)

Don't worry about contacting everyone from your high school band or finding every single bar in a fifty-mile radius that would potentially be cool to play at. Find *one* musician who seems to share your love of your style of music. Find *one* bar. Start small. As you start moving forward, each next step will reveal itself naturally.

When I was building my own company, I came up with a method for keeping track of each next small step. I created a "What's Next?" spreadsheet with two columns (see Figure 2.1). In the first column, I listed all of my projects—for example, "Build website," "Build finance system,"

"Create logo." In the second column, I assigned one task to each project. I never listed more than one because I wanted to focus only on the next step. So next to "Build website," I might have "Research website-hosting companies" in the second column. After I completed that task, I deleted it from the second column and wrote in the next task for the project, for example, "Short-list top three hosting companies." When that was done, I deleted it and wrote "Sign up with GoDaddy web hosting." And so on.

When you focus solely on the next task, the one that follows decides itself. By thinking small like this, you'll avoid feeling overwhelmed and driving yourself crazy. There are a ton of things to do, but you only need to worry about what's next. Dream big—keep that destination in mind—but think small, one step at a time.

WHAT'S IN YOUR WAY? PART 2

In the last track, we addressed personality traits, habits, and mindsets that can get in your way. If you're sleeping past noon and showing up to practice late, scruffy, and confused because you chose drugs over music, you've got to ask yourself, "Do I really want this, man?" That behavior is bullshit and will keep you from reaching your goals.

Another obstacle that derails many musicians is that sneaky little bastard called *fear*. It can keep you from making that phone call, messaging that musician, visiting that club, talking to that bar owner. Overcoming fear is

Project	What's Next?
Build website	Search google for hosting company
Create logo	Call Leandro and setup meeting
Find bass player	Message Greg and ask if he knows anyone
Build a marketing kit	Book photo session on website calendar with Sebastian no later than next week
Improve my visiual performance	Order Tripod from Amazon to setup phone to record
Investment	Fill out form on Ameritrade
Rehearsal Prep	Block four hours in calendar in the next three days to go over my tunes
Band	Video conference with Carla to clear the air about the tension we had—make things better
Relationships	Send a video message to wish Paul a happy birthday

Figure 2.1. "What's Next?" Spreadsheet

key to taking steps toward reaching your goals and making your dreams come true.

Overcoming Fear

When I was seventeen, I went to Steve's Music in Ottawa to pick up some equipment. My friends and I walked in, and I told the dude behind the counter, "I need a Pearl stand for a ride cymbal, please."

Without even looking at me, he said, "We don't have it."

My friends and I looked at each other like *What?*

"Are you sure?" I asked. I could sense that he wasn't telling the truth. He just wanted to get rid of me. As a musician, you know what it's like to really want a piece of equipment. This dude was brushing me off, and I wasn't gonna have it.

At that point, my friends started squirming and walked out of the store, too embarrassed and intimidated to stick around and watch what was about to unfold.

The guy stood his ground. "We don't have it."

"Can you please check your stock?" Don't mistake being courteous and polite for being scared. I know the difference, and so do you.

"We don't have it," he repeated without even checking.

I was done playing nice. "Go in the back and check your stockroom, man."

Then he took it up a notch. "I *said* we don't have it." He was in his mid-twenties and thought that he could intimidate a teenager like me.

He wouldn't move, and I certainly wouldn't take no for an answer. So I asked to see his manager, who upon arrival, made the guy go look for the cymbal stand. He came back with the exact one I had been looking for.

If you love music, there will be times when you have to fight for what you love. Don't take no for an answer or let the fear of confrontation stop you. You will need to be pushy. You will have to act in spite of your fear.

I'm not saying don't be scared. When you try something you've never done before, you probably will feel scared. Feel whatever you feel; that's normal. But don't let that fear stop you from taking action and making things right for everyone involved, starting with you. You'll be amazed at what you can do and how people will agree to help you if you just ask. Plus, if you let fear stop you, you'll be filled with regret someday, thinking of what could have, and would have, been.

Too many people dream big—and then punch that very dream in the gut in one swing. They start telling themselves nonsensical stories about what could happen if they were to take certain actions. For example, when one of my bands was in Beijing, the band leader approached the singer and said, "Hey, some clients in the club want to say hello and to buy you a drink."

She scoffed and said, "I'm not going to whore myself out to anyone."

How did she get from "say hi and buy you a drink" to being whored out? That conclusion stemmed from the stories that she had swirling in her head, which were probably rooted in fear from not being taken seriously as a musician. Somewhere along the line, she started believing that taking certain actions—like saying hello to the fans in the audience—meant she was "schmoozing," selling her soul, and kissing ass. You keep thinking like that, and you're going to end up back at Walmart handing people boxes of chicken legs and wishing you could have said hello to that person when you had the chance. Recognize your fears and ignore those sabotaging stories in your head, so they don't take you down before you really get started.

Today's No Is Tomorrow's Yes

Many people are scared to hear the word *no*, but *no* can't hurt you if you don't let it. We're sometimes so afraid to hear no that we don't even ask the question. How do we know what someone is thinking and how they will respond if we don't ask? We don't. So why not assume that they will say yes instead of no? This will give you the confidence to ask for what you want.

If someone does say no, so what? How do you know that their answer will be no tomorrow? People's circumstances change. That dude who didn't want to be in your band the last time you asked may have had a change of heart for whatever reason. Maybe a bass player's band fell apart, and now he's desperate to join a band just like yours. One day a venue manager may tell you that he doesn't need live bands and then realize that the DJ concept isn't working out and he really does need a live band. Who knows what will happen in this ever-changing world of music and entertainment? To take advantage of any of these opportunities, you have to keep trying. Never give up, whether you hear one or one hundred nos.

One way to turn a no into a yes is to stay in touch with people. You never know when circumstances will change and doors will open. Plus, people know people. If one musician says no, ask if he or she knows someone who wants to join a band—a friend, a relative, a student, anyone. He who turns the most rocks wins. That no today could turn out to be a huge yes tomorrow.

Be Unapologetic

After you figure out what you want, be unapologetic about getting it, no matter what stands in your way. If you're the band leader and you know you want a certain sound that requires a certain skill on the guitar, find that person. If you hire someone who doesn't end up having the skills you want, find someone who does (and nicely let go of the first person; more on that later).

A scene in the movie *I Love You Phillip Morris* has stuck in my head for years as an illustration of this point.

Jim Carrey plays Steven Jay Russell, the newly hired boss. About forty-five minutes into the movie, his beautiful, reserved, and professional assistant comes in and briefs him on the day. Then she asks, "Anything else I can do for you?" to which Steven replies, "Uh, coffee?"

If looks could kill! The assistant glares at him and says, "I'll do that today, but I don't do that really."

Two minutes later, Steven is preparing for a presentation and calls out, "Todd?"

In walks a young, cheerful, energetic young man with a wide smile. To the group in the room, Steven says, "My new assistant, Todd, everybody," and Todd proceeds to help set up the presentation. Just before Steven takes the floor, he says, "Todd, could you get me a coffee? Anybody else want coffee?"

"Yes, sir, right away," Todd replies and walks out.

Carrey's character knew what he wanted: someone to bring him coffee. When the first person wouldn't do it, he found someone else who would—someone who actually enjoyed serving that coffee.

If you hire a musician or singer who ends up not being able to fulfill the vision you have for your band, find someone who can. Don't apologize. Get what you want.

"I WILL NEVER BE FUCKING DEFEATED"

No matter what kind of band you're joining or putting together, or what venue you want to perform at, there's one thing that you can count on happening at some point: you will get rejected.

- That bass player won't return your calls.
- Somebody will tell you that they don't want to work with you.
- Someone will say that you're not good enough of a musician to be in their band.
- Your significant other may tell you, "I don't want you to join that band because I know what that lifestyle is like. If you join, we're done."

When such rejections happen, it's easy to become discouraged. I know, because it happened to me. When I started my first band, when I decided to give up drums and become the main front person, when I started my company—anytime that I started something new, there were days when I just wanted to disappear into a hole because I felt so discouraged and deflated. But I always found a way to keep moving forward. No matter how scared or worried I felt or how many times I failed, I refused to give up. I refused to wallow in self-pity. Instead, I made the next call, sent that email, visited that bar, and walked onstage, knowing that in any one of these acts I might be rejected, laughed at, or judged.

Sometimes when things got very shitty, I would say, "Okay, Georges. You have twenty-four hours to feel all the self-pity you want. Act like a victim, enjoy it, eat chips, watch TV, whine about how it's not fair. Just go for it, man. But when that twenty-four hours is over, get off your ass and get to work."

Being a professional victim is pathetic because no one really cares about your feelings. You will get discouraged and rejected. Just accept that, and get on with it.

Many years later when I was living and working in Bangkok, I finally put words to this mindset that kept me going: "I will never be fucking defeated." I still tell myself this every day because I'm still climbing a mountain, and I'm still moving forward one step at a time. I still hear no. I still get shot down. I still get negative reviews. Every single day.

Remember, you are the only part of this ecosystem that you can control, and you can control how you talk to yourself. "I will never be fucking defeated" doesn't have to be *your* mantra, but find one. You need an inner motor to push you forward when you hit a wall and think about quitting. In reality, your internal dialogue is the difference between winning and losing when it comes to being a successful musician, let alone a successful human. You have to be your own biggest fan.

KEEP THE TRAIN MOVING

There's more than one way to get to the top of a mountain, whether you're talking about a literal slope or a music career. To me, the fastest way to the top is finding people who have climbed before you. Find musicians who have succeeded at a career in music similar to your vision. Ask them questions about what they did first, who they called, where and how they managed to find musicians to join their band, how they approached managers of potential venues to perform at. You still have to do the work, but having someone else's successful journey as somewhat of a road map to follow can make our own journey less stressful and more enjoyable. Whatever you do, keep the train moving, no matter how much fear you feel and how many nos you hear. Just keep moving, one step at a time.

After you figure out what you want and start heading in that direction, it's time to work on the next circle in your ecosystem: the people you're going to play music with.

CHALLENGE

FACE THE FEAR AND DO IT ANYWAY

Is there someone that you would like to call—guitarist, bassist, club owner, bar manager—but you're worried about being rejected? Is there a song that you want to sing in front of people, but you're scared shitless to do so?

Try this: Admit that you're scared. Tell yourself, "I am scared shitless, no doubt about it. I. Am. Scared."

Once that's settled, pick up the phone and call that musician, walk onstage, sing that song. Just do it, despite your feelings. Sure, you may feel rejected, judged, intimidated, even ridiculed! The song may not sound perfect. But at least you know that you defeated your own fears and that you accomplished what you've set out to do. Remember this: the doors to the heavens open to the courageous.

Share what you did even though you were scared, and tag me with #whatsnext #gigforlife.

US

PEOPLE, PEOPLE, PEOPLE

n late 2007, I was on the verge of moving back to Canada to implement the music school business plan that Marc and I had just spent a year and a half creating. Shortly before I was supposed to leave, I had dinner with one of my best friends, Chris Conway, who was the food and beverage director at the Grand Hyatt Singapore, arguably the busiest and biggest money-making live music venue in Asia.

As we ate and enjoyed ourselves, I had an out-of-body experience. I watched myself laugh with Chris and thought, *I like this lifestyle. I could get used to living in Asia and living out loud like this.*

Then I thought, *Why am I going back to Canada?*

The next day, I pulled Chris aside and said, "Bro, I have this idea. I want to manage bands. But I don't want to be an agent." I am and always have been allergic to the word agent because it sounds like some guy who doesn't care about the musicians, the quality of the music, or the bar's success. I explained that I wanted to build bands and set them and their respective venues up for success in every way. I wanted to decide on the band names and appropriate repertoires for each venue and to create each band's look and sound. I wanted to hire musicians from all over the world and match the proper drummer with the proper bass player with the proper singer so that the band would fit like a musical glove.

"How are you going to pull this off?" Chris asked.

"I have no idea, man. But if you get me a contract with Grand Hyatt Singapore, I'll figure it out, and I'll guarantee you that it will be a success."

Chris's reply was simply, "Okay." Chris and I had a history. He knew that I'd put my money where my mouth is, and I wouldn't let him down. I would deliver.

Soon after, I had a gig in Taipei, Taiwan, where I sat down with my great friend and supporter, Olivier Lenoire, who was the food and beverage director at the Grand Hyatt Taipei, and I pitched him my idea. Like Chris, he put his trust in me and said, "Cool, let's do it."

After Taipei, I had a gig at the Sheraton Saigon Hotel in Ho Chi Minh City, Vietnam, where I pitched the same idea to my friend Martin Wuethrich with an added catch: I wanted the gig in Saigon to be my permanent base so that I could continue living and working at the hotel. In other words, I wanted to be the house band. My family and I lived in the suite, which was directly below the club, and it was too noisy for guests. But my band was making all that noise, so it was perfect for us. A few months into the gig, I negotiated an adjacent room for my office.

"I can't play six nights anymore because I have to travel and build the business," I told Martin, "but I'll be onstage three nights a week when I'm in town. I'll give you an amazing discount on all future bands, and I'll come hang out at the club when I'm not playing." That last bit may not seem like a lot, but my presence was important as I had built a huge following. A lot of our guests would come by only if I was at the club, whether I was onstage or just hanging out.

I will never forget the look on his face: part *this is one crazy motherfucker* and part respect for a friend he wanted to help and he believed would deliver. "Okay, Georges, go for it," he said. "I'll support you."

One thing has to be clear: these gentlemen became my friends and said okay so easily because they had seen me year in and year out giving everything I had. Trust had been built because I continually delivered big time.

My family and I ended up living at the Sheraton Saigon Hotel for a total of seven years, until I grew really tired of living in hotels and decided that I wanted my own home, chair, and, as crazy as it sounds, my own coffee cup.

Fast-forward eight months: on July 14, 2008, Chris Conway and I were at the Grand Hyatt Singapore's iconic BRIX club watching my band, Shades, with Mike as the band leader and the amazing Lesley-Ann as lead singer. Meanwhile, Marc's band Xpress hit the stage in Taipei, and Greg did the same in Saigon as the leader of my band, Scarlip. Three bands in three different countries all started their shows at 10:00 p.m. sharp, and just like that, el-live Productions was born.

None of it would have been possible had it not been for the relationships that I had formed and nurtured with all of these amazing people. We respected each other. They knew that I would never mess with their trust, and that I would do everything in my power to deliver on my promise.

Throughout the previous thirty-five years, I have invested in people from many different cultures and backgrounds, musicians, bands, and fans alike, people I treated as friends and family from the moment I met them, people I have kept in touch with regularly. The original members of Scarlip, and Shades before it, became the foundation of el-live Productions. Mike O'Reilly, Marc Lajoie, Greg Lassalle, Rob Varro, Kolette Easy, Lesley-Ann Benjamin, Inga Cossey, Jay Jackson, John Deshennes, Blue Rooney, Sherman Jones II—these are the originals, the guys that I could fully trust. They became the leaders of the founding bands and built the el-live DNA, along with the dynamite Emily Yeh, who assisted with all the nightmare of logistics, and Lesley-Ann, who played two roles as an incredible entertainer–singer and recruitment specialist. They were my eyes, ears, and heart while I was running around from country to country.

To be successful in this business, you have to be a people person. You have to genuinely care about those in your ecosystem: your bandmates, the club owners, bar staff at every level of the operation, your fans. Honestly, if you're not a people person and don't care much about treating others with respect, you need to either learn to become that or get out now.

In this track we'll talk about building and maintaining your team by building genuine, long-lasting relationships.

YOUR DREAM TEAM

Like it or not, whatever you want to do in music involves other human beings, and those human beings have names, lives, and families. They have their own dreams and goals. They have their own personality quirks. These people can facilitate your dreams or make your life very difficult. The key point to remember is that other people's attitudes and actions are never really about you. These people have joined what you're doing because what they want aligns with what you're doing. It suits them and excites them, and they want to be a part of something that they can be proud of. Your combined dreams and vision will enable you to build your team.

You don't need to know a lot of people to have an amazing career in music. You simply need to unite the right people, from musicians to sound engineers to photographers. Finding the right people starts with you being the right person; that's why Set List 1 was all about managing yourself. The secret to being the best version of yourself is being genuine and authentic. Don't bullshit yourself and don't bullshit others. Know from the start that you are one big mess who has things to learn, but you're a wonderful mess, so be kind to yourself.

If you take the time to be authentic and to build genuine relationships, you will have a dream team for a very long time.

HOW TO BUILD LASTING RELATIONSHIPS

Okay, let's get practical. How do you focus on people in your everyday interactions, people who may eventually join your bands or bigger team? Here are some tips for building relationships that last.

Be Supportive

News flash: the people on your team are not there to improve your career. Remember, this is a partnership, one that will benefit the whole ecosystem—musicians, club owners, and fans alike—so make sure you are as support- ive of their dreams as they are of yours.

Being aligned with your team is easier if you work with people who share the same vision and passion: for example, if you're all musicians who want to gig—who, say, love rhythm and blues and strive for a professional career playing live music—then you're already heading in the right direction because you're supporting one another's goals and dreams, which makes things that much easier.

Whenever I hire someone, I'm under the assumption that I'll be working with that person for the rest of my life. Our connection needs to be deeper than just the songs or how we walk onstage. We're all human beings, and we all need to be challenged and fulfilled at a *much* deeper level.

Pay attention. Talk to them. Get to know them. Doing so enables you to understand what their dreams are and how you can help them realize those goals alongside you. One of my company's policies is that we always help out and accommodate our people when need be, even if it's three hundred times in a row. This is what contributes to building lifelong relationships.

However, both parties have to respect the professional relationship as well. Some people may misunderstand and take advantage of the fact that you're supporting their dreams. You must be clear about what aligning their dreams with yours means: the point is to build your band. Their dreams need to align with yours, or none of this will work. If a guy in my band asks if he can hand out business cards to promote himself at our gigs, I'll say, "Hell no!" I didn't bring him into my band to promote his own business. Would I refer him to somebody that could help promote his own music on the side? Of course. But definitely not on our band's time.

Don't Write People Off

During a recent coaching session, I told my coach, "Man, every time I see this one dude in the elevator, I think, *This guy's a dick.* Sometimes he says hello, but other times, he'll ride eleven floors without acknowledging me. It's just him and me, standing in silence."

Then out of the blue one day, the elevator dude said to me, "Hey, do you play golf?"

"Yeah, sometimes," I replied.

So we set a day and played golf and had a fantastic time. It turns out that the guy wasn't a dick at all; he's simply quiet and shy, whereas I'm loud and in your face. Our personalities actually complement each other, and we had a great time the entire day that we played.

Don't judge people based on external appearances and assumptions. If you do, you'll likely miss out on potential friendships with people who really add to your life, and vice versa.

Kill Them with Kindness

When people push my buttons, my nature is to fight back—I don't recommend adopting my nature. Instead, kill people with kindness, no matter how they treat you.

I worked with two managers at two different hotels who seemed determined to do anything in their power to piss me off and make sure I didn't get the gig at their respective hotels. No matter how hard I worked, they complained, so I made it my business to kill them with kindness.

With one of these managers in particular the tension was extreme. Then I found out that his parents had fallen ill. That made me think about how devastated I was when I lost my dad. I had been performing in Asia and was due to travel back to Canada right after the show, but I didn't make it back in time to say goodbye.

So I put aside my feelings and genuinely asked about this manager's parents' health situation. No business motive; I was just honestly extending kindness to him. That act cut through our past differences, and to this day we are wonderful friends. Years later, both managers got me four hotel gigs, which went on for over ten years and paused only during the pandemic. A lot of employed musicians enjoyed a life-changing experience, all because of kindness.

In another situation, I booked one of my bands at a bar that was infamous for its negative staff. Before we ever stepped foot onstage, other bands warned us, "Oh wait till you play there. They have the worst bar staff of any venues we've ever played at. They are entitled, jealous of musicians, and treat us like shit."

We knew that bad staff members could ruin our entire experience. So Mike and I decided to kill the problem with kindness—not just for the sake of being kind, but as a strategy to have success at the club.

We organized a meeting with the staff right away and heard all of their complaints about the other bands: "They played too loud." "They stayed too long." "They left a mess on stage." "They ordered from different servers." On and on. The problems were clear, and Mike addressed each one of them. He told the staff that only one of the musicians would order on everyone's behalf; that not a single glass, towel, water bottle, or piece of trash would be left on stage; and that he would ask them about the volume every couple of days. The staff in general were still not the easiest to work with, but by killing them with kindness, Mike broke through and went on to gig at that club for the next ten years.

Believe You'll Be Friends for Life

Rather than write people off or think, *Well, we're going to do this gig together, and then it's over,* always start off with the presupposition that you'll be friends for life. If you immediately think, *Here's a person I'd like to know for the rest of my life,* you'll behave very differently than if you think that the relationship will be short term. The thought alone creates the opportunity for a lifelong friendship. If you approach people with this mindset, you won't do stupid shit. You won't treat someone poorly because you think that you're not going to see him again. Who knows how you might be able to help this person in the future, or how they might help you?

Give a Lot and Then Some

For as long as I can remember, I have behaved by giving regardless of whether I would receive—just doing good along the way, without expecting anything in return. So when I started my career I did the same thing. I regularly bought a potential bass player a beer and invited band members to my house for drinks, pizza, and conversation.

You might not be comfortable initiating such social events. Or you might be worried about people taking advantage of you—believe me, I've had my fair share of those. But it doesn't compare to the truckload of loyal, giving friends that I've made from being generous. I know without a doubt that if in need, I could pick up the phone right now and have a hundred people here to help me instantaneously.

Don't worry so much about protecting your money, time, and energy. Give and live freely. It will come back in abundance. And remember: generosity doesn't always involve money. You can give time, knowledge, love, or care, which are often more difficult to share. Give in a way that is genuine and right for you, without thinking or worrying about receiving anything in return.

Recognize Milestones in Other People's Lives, Especially the Sad Ones

People are far more forgiving if you skip a wedding or forget a birthday than if you miss a loved one's funeral. Acknowledge people's hard times with a note or a phone call, even if only to say, "Hey, I'm thinking of you." People learn who their real friends are when they're hurting and going through hard times.

Don't Contact People Only When You Need Them

Nothing turns people off like calling them for a favor when they haven't heard from you in years. Stay in touch with people that you meet along your journey. Ask about their families, their work, their hardships. Be a friend.

The thought of keeping track of all these people may seem overwhelming, and you can be certain that your memory will fail you. I recommend that you create a system to help you stay in touch with your friends, acquaintances, and partners. For example, use calendar reminders on your phone to prompt you to touch base every three to six months. When you make that call or type that text, be genuine. If you contact someone with a request, don't beat around the bush. Be up-front about what you need from them and how they can help: "Bro, I'm having a hard time replacing my drummer. Can we meet for a beer? I would like to talk about it."

Because I have a great system in place, I've maintained regular contact with people that I've worked with for more than thirty years. I have kept in touch with those individuals over time, not just in case I need them for favors, but because I care about them and have created and maintained genuine friendships with them. And if I do ever happen to need a favor, I'm up-front about asking. I know that they would be more than willing to help because they know very well that I would do the same for them.

Don't Be Afraid of Confrontation

When something between you and a bandmate is off, sit down as soon as possible and say, "Bro, we have to talk." If you want long-lasting relationships, you have to be honest and straightforward, even if feelings get hurt in the short term. Hiding your true feelings breeds hypocrisy: your bandmate is pissed off, you're pissed off, but you're both smiling at each other like everything is fine. The underlying resentment affects the entire band and ultimately the way that you perform onstage.

Recently, I had lunch with a friend, and I told him why I was pissed off and hadn't been returning his calls. He had no idea that I felt that way. He explained himself and told me that he could see that he was in the wrong and that what he did was not cool. He apologized. At the same time,

I didn't have to give him the cold shoulder. Once I brought the problem out into the open, we were able to move on because we had cleared the air, and there was no more bullshit between us.

When conflict happens, it's best to assume that there is a root cause—something led to this issue that is not so obvious at this minute. Always try to get to that.

Treat Others the Way You Want to Be Treated

This is one of the oldest truths in the world, and it remains valid today. Whether you are confronting someone about their actions or sending them condolences, speak to them the way that you want to be spoken to. Before my lunch meeting with the friend who had pissed me off, I briefed myself: *How would I want someone to talk to me about the shitty thing I just did?* Putting myself in the other person's shoes has saved me more times than I can count.

In another situation, I had to fire someone and I was livid. I could have ripped him apart, but instead I asked myself, *How would I want to be fired?* So I picked up the phone and said, "Bro, you know why I'm calling."

"Yes, G," he said. "You're firing me."

"Yes, I am. You fucked up big time, and you have to go. You are going to end up in jail if you don't change your habits. The team is arranging everything. You have ninety minutes to leave the hotel. Don't mess around. Please don't make me call security."

I spoke to my team and told the band to go say good-bye. I called the guy's mom, even though he was in his late twenties, because he needed to be around his family, and he needed help to get back on track. I told her that her son was on the way home and that if she had any influence over him, she needed to keep him out of Asia so he didn't get himself killed.

A few days later, he called me from home and said, "I love you, G."

"I love you too," I said. "If you need anything let me know, but you will never work with me again."

I was up-front with this guy from the beginning, no beating around the bush, because that's the way I would want to be treated if I was getting fired.

The same is true on the other side: if you fuck up, acknowledge it right away. And if your fuck-up happens in public, do not apologize in private. If you say something in front of three other people, then you have to apologize in front of the same people. I certainly would expect a public apology—wouldn't you?

Another note on this subject: when you need to talk to someone about an issue, don't say, "Hey, we need to talk," and then leave them hanging for a day or two. How do you feel when someone does that to you? It gives you a heart attack, right? So don't do that to others. Instead, say something like "Hey, I'd like to talk to you. It's not urgent. I just want to ask you about X." Always be considerate in your communication with others and handle it the way you would want them to handle it with you.

Don't Air Your Dirty Laundry on Social Media

You will get pissed off at your partners—I can guarantee it—but keep the disagreement "in the family." Never get in a comment war with your bandmates on social media. Not only is it classless, but you never know how it might affect your immediate and future relationships.

I once watched a fight unfold in real-time comments on Facebook. The person who aired the dirty laundry never mentioned the musician's name, but people knew who he was talking about. Not a good idea. If you're the one airing the dirty laundry, other musicians will now know that you will not hesitate to assassinate their character in front of the whole world when you have beef with them. Who wants to work with someone like that and take that kind of a chance? No one.

If you think social media is your platform for private expression and it's nobody's business, you're wrong. The first thing people do, in this business and in any other line of work, is check out your online presence. My company does, and I can assure you that if you have a reefer in your hand and you're sticking the middle finger out to the world with a grin in every post, you ain't catching a ride on the el-live train, because in countries like Singapore, they don't find that cute. They will lock you up and throw away the key, and no one from the outside can help, so keep your drama for your mama and think long and hard before you post on social media.

Get Familiar with the Leaders

In every walk of life, there are individuals who are natural leaders of the pack, guys who can move mountains. Chris Conway was an influencer way before the term became a social media buzzword. If he said, "Give Georges a gig," Georges got the gig.

Learn to recognize the influencers around you, and nurture those relationships. They're not idiots. They know their position. They're well aware of the power that their reputation carries, and they most likely expect to be "used" along the way. One day I flat-out told one of these leaders, who was also a friend, that I dropped his name everywhere I went in order to get gigs.

"I know," he said. "Knock yourself out."

Even though they expect it, be up-front about it. Be genuine, forthcoming, and honest. Know who the influencers and leaders of the pack are at a human level, as well as at a musician's and bar-owner's level. They will open so many doors for you.

Every group of people that comes into a bar was led there by one person—the leader, the one the group turns to when they can't make a decision. These are the people who will bring ten more people next Friday night. Be aware of who they are, and bring them into your ecosystem.

Don't Burn Any Bridges

Even if you get your shit together and treat people right, some people will exit your life. It happens. People are allowed to try something new. Musicians try new bands, bar owners hire new entertainment, band leaders seek new singers or guitar players. There may even come a time when you decide to quit to try something new.

Whether you're the person leaving or being left, be professional. If a bar owner doesn't renew your contract or if your drummer decides to try another band, don't be bitter and bad-mouth them. Don't take it personally. You might be in the same position someday.

In addition, you never know when you might meet these people again. Years down the road, you may discover that you have mutual connections in the business or that they're part of a band that performed right before you. Wherever you go, your reputation comes along. It never leaves you. When you cross paths again with people from the past, you'll be glad that you didn't burn that bridge.

One day while in Tokyo, I walked into a bar and ran into some old friends from Abu Dhabi. The music business is the smallest in the world, and maintaining those connections can work in your favor.

Maintain Your Team

Building and maintaining your team is the most important action that you can take after working on yourself. The truth is, you will not achieve your goals in a music career if you don't consider everyone else's dreams and aspirations as well. This is a partnership. You are working together to gig for life. Start working on your relationships now, and be a genuine, authentic person in all of your interactions.

Over the years, your ecosystem will grow. You will work with photographers, graphic designers, musicians, bar owners, and more. Figure 3.1 shows a map of all the people I have met during my career. Some of these relationships have lasted the whole thirty-plus years that I've been a professional musician because I always made it a priority to maintain my team. This business is all about the people that you grow it with, so you should keep track of who they are and treat them right.

After you have your team in place, it's important that everyone knows their position. Properly structuring your band from the get-go is key to running it like a real business, which we cover next.

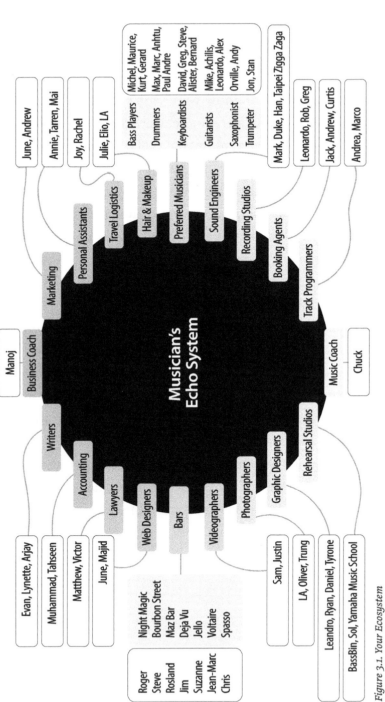

Figure 3.1. Your Ecosystem

CHALLENGE

REACH OUT

Make a list of all the people that you know, then contact them one by one. Write an email, send a text, call them—whatever works for you. Tell them that you just wanted to say hi, or thank them for something that they did as recently as last week or even ten years ago, or express how much you appreciate their friendship.

One day I was in a cab in China when someone who had worked with me years earlier called me out of the blue. I was so happy to hear from him.

"Georges," he said, "I am calling to say I'm sorry. I was an asshole when we worked together."

"It's cool, man," I said. "It's forgotten." Then we talked, reminisced, and giggled. Sadly, two months later he passed away. I was happy we had made peace first.

Don't wait until you're facing your final days before reaching out to people who have helped you, or who you may have hurt along the way. This life is all about people, people, people, so make them a priority every day.

Show appreciation for someone on social media, and tag me with #people #gigforlife.

THE BAND IS A BUSINESS

When I started my first band, According to Roger, my bandmates and I were all studying music at Concordia University in Montreal: myself on drums, Roger Sagous (aka Sage) on keys, Mike O'Reilly on guitar, Kirt Xavier on bass, and Janis Thompson as lead singer.

We were all very young. We had some colorful disagreements, but we made it work for a while, five years to be exact, mainly because we liked each other and compromised a lot.

Many of our issues came about because our band had no clear leader. We were friends who were excited to be part of a band. The vibe was right, so why mess with it?

Most bands start the same way. It's like dating: everyone is in love and on a huge high, so no one sees a need to set ground rules about how the band is going to run. It never dawned on me to systematically put a structure in place and make the leadership official, even though I had founded the band, hired all the musicians and agents, booked all the gigs, negotiated deals—all the important activities that a business owner normally does.

What did I learn from approaching our band this way? Plan your divorce and sign on the dotted line when you're in love, because things can get very ugly when people are bitter.

When there's no leader, everyone feels free to share *lots* of opinions, which brings everything to a halt when people disagree. I was the only person in our band who had any business experience, but we still had many debates on how many things should be done, how to best negotiate gigs, how to design pamphlets—you name it. I accommodated the others, but on the inside I became very frustrated. No one meant any harm—they were just participating—but discussing so many opinions really slowed down the decision making.

In business and in life, nothing is ever fast enough for me. I want to do everything yesterday, so this slow pace drove me insane, but I still let it go on for five years.

We were already working nonstop when we finally landed a house gig in Old Montreal at a club called Nuit Magique (Night Magic). For two years we played there seven days a week with two full gigs on Saturday and Sunday, one during the day and another one at night. Janis couldn't be with us all the time because she was raising her son and the schedule was grueling, so Derek Martin filled in on vocals. He was from Detroit and brought the whole package—the voice, the charm, the showmanship.

The bar owner was a great guy, but his brother was a jackass. He worked at the bar and treated the band like shit. So me being me, I walked up to the owner one day and told him how his brother was treating us. He said okay and was seemingly supportive. Behind my back, however, he started putting together another band. One day I woke up and the gig at Nuit Magique was gone, and Mike had somehow been convinced to join the new band. We worked our butts off and truly packed the joint for two years straight, and the gig was taken away without any discussion.

I was disgusted and bitter. I wanted nothing more to do with running a band, so I broke up According to Roger, and we all went our own ways.

Terrible things can happen when you don't have clear leadership and structure to your band. People get hurt. You can lose friends. Even though those years had been some of the best in my life, they were also extremely stressful. After the band broke up, I didn't talk to Mike for a year and a half, and we had been really close friends. Even worse, one of the band members took his own life. I'm convinced the breakup of the band and breaking up with his girl-friend played a big part in his extreme unhappiness.

After taking a break for about a year and a half, I took a couple of gigs as a musician, not as a leader. It was nice to simply focus on the music again but tough to see mistakes and not be able to fix them. Because of my relationships with bar owners, they still approached me with questions and concerns as if I was the band leader. I couldn't avoid it.

One day I went to see Janis, who was playing with a funk band in a club on St. Laurent Street. They were good. No, they were *amazing*. A few times in my life, I've had an out-of-body experience when I know I have no choice but to follow the calling. This was one of those times. I left the joint knowing I needed to start a funk band.

By then Mike and I were talking a little. We had been great friends and had worked together for so long, and we both felt an emptiness. Mike didn't have a great experience with the other band. Even though the musicians were some of the best in Montreal, they didn't share his values—just like the bands I tried really didn't share mine. Besides, I couldn't think of anyone better for the funk concept than Mike, because he is funky as hell and I loved the way he played.

This time, though, I did it right. My scars were fresh, and I wasn't about to make the same mistakes twice, for my sake and for everyone's sake, so Mike and I had a meeting and I laid down the structure: I was going to be the leader of the band. We would discuss all of the issues and new hires, but in the end, I would make all of the final decisions. I had a clear vision of what I wanted to do with the band, and to remove any doubt of who was in charge, I gave the band my family name: Elchakieh.

Then I hired the best in the funk style, starting with the amazing band I saw on St. Laurent. Yeah, I hired all of them: Dany Blanco, Dorothy Clark, Dessy De Lauro, Alan Prater, David Edmead, Michel Belanger, and Janis from According to Roger, as well as my future wife, Julie. With the new structure, I was free to execute my vision and move quickly. Everyone knew their roles and embraced them, and we kicked royal ass.

The structure of any band has to be clear. Activities like getting paid, finding gigs, scheduling rehearsals, organizing transportation—who takes care of these things? Who pays for the expenses? Who makes the final decision? What I'm about to say here will sound controversial, but it's true: your band is not a democracy. You don't have time to vote and wait for a unanimous decision. You'll end up spending three hours discussing what type of paper to print your fliers on or whether rehearsals should be at 3:00 or 4:00.

Like it or not, if you're seeking to make a living from your music, you have to run your band as a business—or join one that is run like a business. In either case, somebody has to be the boss. I would never join a band, company, or any institution that did not ultimately have a CEO, a president, or a boss, regardless of the title. This does not mean you should be a tyrant or not listen to anyone's opinion or not discuss issues, but do yourself and everyone else a favor and lead, or get out of the way.

In this track, we'll talk about what makes your business a business, the importance of determining who's the boss, and two key parts of running your band as a business: structure and people management.

YOUR BAND IS A BUSINESS, PERIOD

I can hear the objections now: "I am an artist, man. My band is not a business." Okay, fine, be an artist and don't ask for money. But the minute money gets exchanged, your band becomes a business. You're going to pay people to play in your band. You're going to pay someone to engineer the sound and someone to move you and your gear from here to there. You're going to get paid for playing in a club. Basically, your music is a service for sale.

Call it art, call it an organization, call it a spiritual endeavor, call it whatever you want to make yourself feel better about it, but the fact remains: when money gets exchanged, it's a business. No matter what descriptions you use, the activities—marketing, payroll, accounting, logistics—are part of being a business.

Some musicians think that considering their music and their band as a business is beneath them. They don't realize that in many ways, playing at a wedding or at a bar is no different from any day job. If you work at Best Buy, you're required to wear a certain uniform and greet people in a certain way so that you can collect that paycheck every two weeks. Don't you wear a certain "uniform" to your gigs—jeans and a T-shirt with rolled-up sleeves or a tuxedo if you play at a formal event? And don't you follow a predetermined set list of songs in order to collect your pay at the end of the night? Like it or not, that's a business.

This business of your band is going to happen with or without you. Money will be exchanged. People will be hired and fired. A service will be provided poorly or professionally. It's happening. Better recognize it and embrace it, so you can put systems in place to make the process go as smoothly as possible.

WHO'S THE BOSS?

Before we talk about business management, you need to determine your role in the band.

When you join or start a band, you hold one of two roles: a supporter/member or the boss. Before you enjoy the rest of this track, figure out which role you hold.

If you're a supporter, you probably won't need to worry about creating the business structure of your band. You can voice your opinion and provide helpful insights, but ultimately the boss has the final say. Your role as a supporter is to believe in and adopt the structure implemented. If you don't want to be part of the established structure, why join? You'll only be setting yourself and the band up for problems. Look for another band that has a structure you align with.

If you're the boss, that means you decide where to play, how much everyone gets paid, who is hired and fired, and more. You are responsible for setting up a structure from the beginning. You also need to learn to manage characters and egos from day one.

If you're the boss, then be the boss, no apologies. That doesn't mean you should be a tyrant. Be a leader, set expectations up front, and follow through; in many ways, it's that simple.

One other option sometimes is to be a co-leader, but I don't recommend this. It's like having two presidents leading a country. Sooner or later, you will have a falling out.

BUILD A SANCTUARY

Whether you're the boss or a supporter, do yourself a favor and build a sanctuary—a place where you can work, practice, listen to music, be creative, and relax. Make it cozy and comfortable, the place you want to be more than anywhere else. Bring in your favorite chair. Decorate it with plants or music posters. Do whatever you need to do to make it a place of refuge that puts you in a calm, creative mindset.

STRUCTURE

I've made many mistakes in my life, and being wrong about the structure of my first band is one of them. It cost me mental and emotional well-being for a long time. Now I've got everything down to a science. I decide what the band's style is, what kind of music we play, how often we play, what songs we'll sing, how many rehearsals we have, and how much everyone gets paid. If you're the boss, you'll need to do the same.

Many times you will personally lose a lot of money, and no one will say thank you for the sacrifice; so be it. Other times you'll make money, as you should; you earned it. Don't complain when you lose money and don't apologize when you make money, either. Ultimately, as the leader, you're the one that takes the most risk. People will argue with you about the money or profit, but when unforeseen events happen—the band van breaks down, a bar owner doesn't pay—all of a sudden you become the boss real fast with zero opposition, and it's your problem to fix.

How you handle finances, hiring and firing, marketing, dress code, and more all stem from three foundational pieces: your purpose, values, and promise.

Purpose

Purpose is why you wake up in the morning. It's who you are at the deepest level. It's your soul, your belief system, the reason your heart beats, your raison d'être. Making your band into a business gives that heartbeat a rhythm. It keeps the whole organism healthy and running optimally.

For years I knew that I was happiest when everyone around me was happy, but I didn't think of this as my purpose until recently. Now I know this is my reason for being. It's why I started playing music. It's the heartbeat behind my business, el-live Productions. In fact, our stated purpose as a company is to make somebody happy, to be the most exciting part of people's days, and to build a community of musicians and music lovers.

So what is your purpose? What makes you happy? What excites you? What gives you a sense of fulfillment? If you're like me, you're probably already acting in line with your purpose; you just haven't really articulated it. Take time to really think about what gets you out of bed every morning.

If you don't feel your purpose as a musician in every bone of your body, you'll never be able to convince anybody to do anything. Yes, you need to set up all the business pieces covered in this track, but the business is just the structure to bring your purpose, your passion, and your dream to life.

Purpose will keep you going when you have to make hard decisions, when things get tough and you have to find new venues or new bandmates. It's why you wanted to start this crazy journey in the first place. You have to start here. Your purpose will inform your values and brand promise and the rest of the structure.

Values

If purpose is why we wake up in the morning—the reason for being—values are the rules and regulations involved in how we conduct business to align with our purpose. They are the dos and don'ts that guide your actions, day by day, gig by gig.

Determining your values is a lot like setting up your brand promise. Instead of asking yourself what you want to deliver, ask yourself, *What's important to me, and how do I want the people in my band to act?*

Every time I advise band leaders on hiring new band members, I apply value to it: "Don't tell them what to do. Don't tell them what not to do. Ask yourself, *Can this person align with our values?*"

Let's say one of your band's big values is "We take care of each other," and one of your bandmates is sick. Do you and the rest of the guys go visit her? Do you call her? Do you bring her medicine? Tea? If not, do you think she's going to take care of you the next time you need something? Your values must speak through your actions—onstage and in every area of life—before you expect them from your band members.

If you're the boss, your job is to hire people who already share your values, not hire people and then teach them your values. You might create values that don't reflect where you really are right now, but where you want to go. Even still, the people you hire should be of the same mind, have the same goals. Make no apologies about what your values are. Use them to better yourself and your bandmates.

If someone seems like a good fit at first but has behavior issues down the road, you can use values to address the issue: "This behavior doesn't align with our values." As the boss, you may need to repeat this till you're blue in the face: "This is not who we are and how we do things. It's nothing personal, but this isn't working out." It's that simple. When you remember your band is a business, it takes a lot of the hurt feelings out of the equation.

Promise

A brand promise is not the same as a tagline like "I'm lovin' it," "Just do it," or "Simply great." The brand promise is what you guarantee to the customer. An airline's brand promise is that you're not going to die in the air. Walmart's is essentially "We have the cheapest price, or we'll match it." For a pizzeria, it's usually something like "We'll deliver your pizza in thirty minutes or it's free." When purpose and values align, delivering on your promise will be natural. It will flow from what you do and say.

If a bar owner asks you, "Why should I hire your band?" he is essentially asking for your brand promise: what do you guarantee to give him and his customers?

If you have thought this through ahead of time, you'll be ready. You could say, "I promise, if you hire my band, not a single one of your customers will be passive when we start playing. They will all be engaged, arrive twenty minutes early and stay twenty minutes after the show, and even come on Thursdays because we're going to create a vibrant atmosphere. That means more drink sales for you."

Another brand promise might be this: "We're going to create an atmosphere that envelopes the room. People can still have a conversation and enjoy each other's company. Our band will fill all the awkward silences on first dates and keep the night interesting."

A wedding band might say, "Both Grandma and little Johnny will have a great time. We'll play the groom and bride's favorites throughout the night at a volume level that is acceptable for everyone."

My band's brand promise is "Every night is Saturday night." We play six nights a week, and I tell bar owners and audience members alike, "I promise you that if you come on a Monday, you're going to see the same show you would at the height of the weekend. You're not going to see a Monday night show or a Wednesday night show; you're going to see *the* show."

To emphasize the importance of brand promise with my band, we regularly record videos of our performances and then review with all of the musicians. If I have to point out a mess-up or give a shout-out, I can point to the video and say, "Look. Thank you so much for doing that. This goes straight with our brand promise" or "See this?

That's not who we are or how we do things in this band. Now let's fix it."

Everything else falls into place when you structure your band around purpose and a promise right from the start. Every single musician should know and live out your brand promise. If they don't, find someone else. No one's talent is so amazing that you have to keep them around when they don't live out your brand promise—not even someone like Midnight Dave.

FINANCES

When I started creating and leading bands in the late 1980s, many musicians felt the band leader should be paid the same as everyone else. I disagree. For every hour a supporting musician works, the boss puts in twenty more, which doesn't include the hours of stress and worry. It's the leader's name that's on the line. If the band screws up the gig, the guitar player can go back to that gig with another band, but the leader can't. He's the one in charge, so he will take the brunt of the blame. He's the one risking everything.

As the boss, you're responsible for negotiating the price and deciding how much each person is paid. After you work it out, be up-front and ask each person, "Is this amount good for you?" If they agree, that's it. End of discussion. If someone wants to negotiate, you can pay them more if you can afford it. If not, the person has the choice to walk away. You can always find another musician. Side note: if you are a musician and you agreed to the price, don't go back to renegotiate. The band leader won't trust you next time. If you feel you should have negotiated better, learn your lesson and do better the next time around.

In addition, as the boss you are under no obligation to share how much you're making on the gig, same as any other boss in any other business. Likewise, don't feel obligated to share what each person in the band is making. They will not all deserve the same amount. Some people are more talented, some are more committed, some may have joined a year ago while others joined yesterday, some pull in customers and others have zero effect on the crowd. Be very clear with each individual about what their salary is, and pay them what you promised, on time, all the time. By "on time" I mean at the end of the gig. Never ever pay anyone early, ever, because then they will be coming to you to pay them early all the time. At the same time, never pay them a minute late.

NEVER TOO YOUNG

Some of you might be in college. You might be thinking all this talk about structure and finances and marketing is way over your head. Not true. My son is a successful YouTuber (yes, it's a thing). He just turned nineteen, and he owns a registered corporation with copyrighted logos. He has a legal team—a tax attorney, a corporate lawyer, and a copyright lawyer—as well as an agent and an accountant, and he hires freelancers to handle functions such as graphic design, editing assistance, camera crews, merchandise campaigns—the list goes on. He also started investing from the very first paycheck he received.

I do like bragging about my son, but the main reason I share this is to show you that you can do it too. I took what I learned about business over the last forty years and taught it to my son over the course of seven months, and now he is rocking his business. All of the stuff I'm sharing with you—it works, *if* you work the system.

MARKETING

Marketing has come a long way since I started doing it. In the 1980s and '90s, we used word of mouth, handed out pamphlets, stapled posters to phone poles, and dropped off flyers in cafes, restaurants, and supermarkets. Now you can post on Facebook, Instagram, or Tiktok, and suddenly, twenty thousand people know what you're doing. Social media can be very helpful in promoting your next gig.

Even though marketing is relatively easy now, I've heard musicians say, "My job is to play music at a bar.

Now I've got to market for them too? What else am I going to do? Serve the beer?"

You don't *have* to do anything. Just understand this: if you do something, there's a consequence; if you don't do something, there's a consequence. Where you fall short gives other bands room to grow—room on the stage at the bars where you want to play.

Marketing is exactly how I staked my claim on the local bars in my area: I did all the work other bands didn't want to do. I designed and printed posters. I went to bars and talked to people about our gigs. When social media became a thing, I posted on social media. Because I put in the work, I brought in big crowds who bought a lot of drinks and made the bar owners a lot of money. Then I delivered on my brand promise every single time. Every night was Saturday night. As a result, I decided where and when I played, and I was able to name my price. The other bands lost out, and then they complained to the bar owners: "Why the fuck are you paying Georges thousands of dollars a weekend?"

The answer was simple: value, brother. Value.

BOOKING GIGS

In the next track I'll cover booking in a lot more detail, but here's a demo for you.

To book the gig, you first have to ask yourself, "What's in it for the bar owners?" and then pitch your band based on that answer.

Many musicians make the big mistake of telling a bar owner, "We're great! My singer is fantastic! Here's my long, boring resume." What does that do for the owner, who is probably thinking, *Rent is coming up—are these guys going to bring in crowds who buy drinks?*

Instead of focusing on me, me, me (we've played that track, remember?), you might say, "We have a following. I guarantee that your audience will be very entertained. They will stay longer and come back tomorrow. I know so-and-so; they can vouch for me." Now the owner can see how they might benefit.

DRESS CODE

The two biggest complaints we get on a regular basis are the repertoire and wardrobe. Bar owners care a lot about both. We'll talk about songs and set lists later, so let's consider your wardrobe for now.

Dressing appropriately for the music and venue adds to the atmosphere. You can play the best music anyone's ever heard, but if you don't look the part, you won't get a second gig at that joint. As suggested in the next track, you should visit the venue before you play there to find out what the crowd wears. Follow the same theme, but kick it up a notch. You may be wearing a cowboy hat and jeans like most of the audience, but your outfit should look designed, manicured, and a bit over the top. A few more rhinestones, hipper jeans, a cooler hat.

Here's one way to look at it: if someone sees you walking in the audience, they should immediately get the feeling that you are in the band. In other words, you should stick out like a sore thumb in a cool way. If you don't, your wardrobe probably doesn't have enough pizzazz for the stage. Think of Dexter Gordon, Miles Davis, and James Brown—they killed it with their style. Prince and David Bowie took it to the next level.

Even if you're a rocker with jeans and a T-shirt, that look should appear artistic, like it belongs onstage. Don't wear your day clothes for a gig. They don't scream fun, special, or professional. I would be scared shitless if my doctor walked in with running shoes, baseball cap, tattoos, shirt unbuttoned to his navel and said, "Okay, let's open this sucker up and patch those arteries," while Nirvana is blasting in the background. I want him to look like a professional, with a white coat and a name tag. Even though he is the same talented and brilliant doctor, his appearance is part of what makes me trust him. It's no different on the stage. Dress the part of a musician who is ready to bring on one hell of a show. Your appearance contributes to the overall vibe and affects the way people experience the music.

Also, empty your pockets before a show. Better yet, cut them out and sew them shut so you get a clean, smooth look that elongates your frame. The faded outline of your wallet in your back pocket is not very hip; neither are pockets sticking their ears out or crumpled fabric poking through your T-shirt when you move around onstage. Cut 'em out.

Part of being the boss is deciding and enforcing the uniform for your business. For about five years, my band wore either all black or black and white. We tried the color theme as well, with everyone showing up in red or blue, but it ended up looking cheesy. We have now moved on to color palettes, and I created a document with vivid pictures for reference. For example, a fall color scheme would have everyone wearing something that had orange, dark orange, light brown, or green. We now rotate about seven palettes, so no matter what the band members have in their closet, something will fit in the color scheme for the night.

One hint if you use palettes: if you are working five to seven nights a week, make sure you don't use the same number of palettes as nights, because you'll end up wearing the same thing every Monday, which means the Monday crowd is going to see the same outfits every week. Our bands play six nights a week, so we rotate seven palettes: palette one on the first Monday and palette seven on next Monday.

Even if you use the color palette method, do the Costco check: your friends should look at you and say, "Bro! Isn't this a bit much just to grab some groceries?" You should stand out if you walk in the store wearing your stage-time wardrobe.

PEOPLE MANAGEMENT

A psychologist knows what her job is. So does a truck driver, a lawyer, a doctor, and a nurse. They all know what is expected of them in the workplace.

In bands, the reason egos get out of hand is that people don't know their place. Musicians are walking, breathing paradoxes. They are confident and insecure at the same time. They are disciplined in one area but erratic in another. They will defend themselves to the very end, knowing that everyone knows that they're full of shit. They'll even risk getting fired because in their mind, they're the next big talent.

Playing with other musicians is what we love. The comradery, the laughs, teasing each other—it's a beautiful thing with memories that you will cherish forever. But managing those same musicians can also be a huge headache. This is another area where you need to make some decisions up front and communicate them clearly from the start. I learned that the hard way when I hired a singer a while back. Before one show, I asked her to dance during the performance, and she said, "I refuse to dance." Soon after, she got a gig with another band, and I went to watch them play. That singer was dancing her ass off!

"Why wouldn't you do that in my band?" I asked her afterward.

"The band leader made it clear from the beginning that if I wanted the gig, I had to dance onstage," she said simply.

I didn't do that, and I paid the price. Make your expectations clear from the start.

Once you have the structure set up, your job is to understand the people you bring in and manage them professionally. To find the best way to handle one moment to the next, you've got to figure out each member's personality traits, tendencies, strengths, and weaknesses—and learn to find something you like in every person you meet.

Personality Traits

Don't let anyone tell you that there's no such thing as a generalization; that's really not accurate as a blanket statement. Different cultures behave in different ways and have different preferences. Based on my experience, even provinces and cities can differ in behavior, tastes in music genres, clothing, food—you name it. There are cultural differences between the French and the Irish, the Vietnamese and the Thais. That's what makes each group so wonderful and travel so magical. However, the differences are 100 percent undeniable.

There are certain things that you can generalize about musicians too: drummers behave a certain way, and so do singers, bass players, and the rest. Based on my experience and the many musicians I have worked with, it's like the nature of the instrument and its demands can have a direct correlation to personality traits, as if your personality adjusts to your instrument's demands.

Let's take two musicians as an example, the extremes: the one up front, with the smallest instrument, the mic, and the one way in the back with the biggest instrument, the drum set.

Singers know intrinsically that they *are* the show. They're right up front, what everyone in the audience is looking at. They're the band's main draw in attention and in cash and they know it, and that confidence comes with a certain attitude that can be either good or not so good, depending on the singer.

In my thirty-plus years of hiring musicians, only two singers have shown up with their own mic. *Two!* Most expect the club or band leader to bring it for them. Can you imagine the bass player or drummer making that assumption? No. But, it's really not the singer's fault. It's the nature of the instrument. The rest of the band is behind him, and he is, in many ways, carrying the success of the show. It's a huge responsibility: that person has 99 percent of the room staring at them 99 percent of the time. Many singers can let it get the best of them and behave like it's all about them.

In addition, most singers are naturally talented and can practice while driving, walking around the house, or cooking. The nature of the instrument does not force them to sit down and systematically learn the tune or practice. Learning a tune is hard work, for sure, like any other instrument, but it's not confining and it doesn't take a lot of setup time, designated space, or strict discipline. Practice can be more free flowing.

Also, because they get most of the adulation as well as scrutiny, singers can become a bit nutty, overconfident, jealous, and insecure all at the same time. The nature of the instrument and their position in the band can put them on an emotional roller coaster, which explains why there is often great tension between singers and musicians. Musicians think that a lot of singers are flakes, and singers think, *The show is nothing without me anyway, so who cares what the musicians think.* The debates between musicians and front singers can be entertaining as hell.

What about drummers? We have all heard the ten million drummer jokes, like "Hey, what do you call the guy who hangs out with musicians? A drummer." It's funny—but this couldn't be further from the truth. In general, I've found that drummers have their shit together more than any other musician; this is why most of the leaders in the bands I've formed are drummers. They are generally the most responsible because they have the most invested. To even get started, they have to pay four to five thousand dollars to buy a drum set. Then they have to rent a place to practice and have a car for transportation. You can't just call a taxi and throw your drum set in the trunk.

Drummers also have a lot invested time-wise. Because they have a car, they are often the designated taxi for the rest of the band. They show up at the bass player's house, and he's running five minutes late. Multiply that by five, and the drummer is leaving ninety-plus minutes before the rehearsal or gig, because after he picks everyone up, he still needs a good forty minutes to assemble his set once they arrive. I think most musicians would agree that the drums are in a league of their own as far as setup and teardown. Also, out of all the bands we have built and managed, drummers don't seem to get sick, and if they did, they wouldn't be able to take a day off because most of the time there would be no show. The band cannot play without the drummer, so they deal with it and show up because the show must go on.

Are all singers prima donnas? Of course not, but many can be. Are all drummers the poster child for responsibility? No, though I would say most are. The bottom line is, the better you know your band members in general and their individual personalities and what can make them behave in a certain way, the better you can run your business.

There are all types of musicians. You can't put the same pressure on everyone. Some are extroverts like me, and some are shy and not outgoing at all. Marc was shy. I helped out by introducing him to the crowd or a table of people. I'd take that burden off of him by leading and initiating for him.

Some musicians are talented, but they have a hard time learning their parts. They just can't sit down and go over the music or lyrics. So I assign people who are very organized and whose strength is learning songs to help those who struggle. Other musicians can learn the words easily but have a hard time with the presentation onstage. The singer might be able to help out here. Matching people's challenges and strengths is a great way to build comradery, which is essential to building a successful band.

BANDS ARE BUILT OFFSTAGE

Bands are built offstage, during the time when you're not performing or rehearsing. Get to know the humans behind the instruments by hanging out after rehearsals or having coffee or going for a walk and talk. Ask questions about your bandmates' families, their interests outside of music, where they grew up, and where they like to vacation.

When musicians are friends and love each other, the audience can feel it and that adds to their experience of the show. That kind of connection requires an investment of time and energy, and most of the time that takes place offstage. But that investment is worth it.

When you put in the effort, you build a solid base so that when hiccups and conflicts happen—and they will—your band members will have each other's backs and be more supportive and understanding. If the relationships are not built and nurtured beforehand, the smallest issues can become major problems, which will negatively affect the show you give your audience. However, if you invest in those relationships offstage, you can work together powerfully onstage to give the audience something magical. Plus, it is so much fun to work with people you know and love!

Incident vs. Tendency: Know the Difference

When you're managing people, it's important to know the difference between isolated incidents and ongoing tendencies. For example, if someone is always late for rehearsal or complains about something at every gig, that's a tendency that needs to be addressed. However, if it's a one-time thing, don't make a big deal out of it. Just give them a hug and say, "Bro, don't do that anymore." Then let it go. Save your energy for tendencies, not incidents.

One tendency you need to especially watch out for is the shit-stirrer. As the band leader, you might say, "Does anyone have anything to say?" The shit-stirrer will say, "No, no. Everything's cool." The minute everyone leaves, however, they go have a coffee with the most vulnerable member of the group and talk shit about another band member or a decision you made. Make sure these people have no place in your band.

Fire the Shit-Stirrers

If you're the band leader who has clear, nonnegotiable values, at some point you're going to have to fire someone. When that time comes, you'll probably be tempted to put it off or make excuses like, "I need to find a replacement first." Don't do it. You know in your gut when you need to fire someone, so just do it. Don't wait for a replacement. The longer you wait, the more shit they're going to stir.

That said, make sure people know why they're being fired. If you have been clear about your expectations all along, and direct and candid about when people aren't measuring up, then people won't be blindsided when they're let go. They'll actually expect it.

For example, if one of the guys talks behind people's backs, I call him up and say, "We don't allow this. We don't allow cliques." Then I give him a chance to express himself and share his side of the story. Sometimes the issue ends there. If it happens again, I tell him, "This is the second time we've talked about this. The next time you hear my voice on this issue it will be the last."

If they keep it up, then I follow through. When I call, they already know what it's about. I say, "It's nothing personal, but our values don't seem to align. We don't seem to have the same purpose, and we don't seem to be able to deliver the promise we agreed on and you were hired for."

We send them out with all the respect in the world. I pay for their plane ticket and check on them afterward.

That's another principle in our company: "Love them on the way in. Love them on the way out."

People always feel they are mistreated when they are fired, so I make sure to treat them right. Because of that, we actually have more musicians sent to us by people we've fired than people we don't have issues with.

If possible, it's best to have this tough conversation in person. If you can't fire them in person, then do it over a video call. They need to see that you aren't a coward. Look them in the eye, and let them know why they're being fired. Then send them on their way, holding no grudges. Love them on the way in. Love them on the way out.

Whatever you do, don't waver when someone needs to be fired. I've only wavered once, and I still regret it. He was a shit-stirrer and ended up breaking up the band. Fire these guys first, and fast. Never wait for a replacement. If he has to go, let him go right away, and then take care of step two: finding a replacement. Even though it may be inconvenient for a while, everyone will thank you for it.

There was a time when I had a few shit-stirrers in a few different bands. I woke up every morning with fear in my gut, thinking, *God...which customer am I apologizing to today? Who am I reprimanding today?* It seemed like someone was always doing something stupid over the seven hours I was in bed. I was worn out from the constant complaints and from the calls we made to say, "Bro, please stop. This is not going to end well for anyone" or "Hey, girl, don't get stupid drunk and hit your fellow singer."

During our next team meeting, I said to Emily, "Please go through every single email, note, and message and give me a list of every motherfucker who has been complained about in the last year. I want to—"

Before I even finished, Emily was at the computer, making a list. Emily was just as pissed as I was and tired of getting the same 4:00 a.m. phone calls about so-and-so causing problems. When she handed me the list, I said, "Fire them all. Today."

I had the logistics team ready. We booked flights and called the hotels. I had the band leaders go to these individuals' rooms and give them ninety minutes to pack their bags and be in the car waiting outside. I called housekeeping and had them return their dirty laundry. They got their plane tickets, their last paycheck, and they were gone.

It was a surgical strike, like the cops doing a drug bust. All at once, there was a great exodus of assholes across eleven different countries. And the next morning, I had zero emails.

Here's the kicker: *nobody* told me that I should not have done that—not one leader or musician. Everybody who contacted me afterward thanked me for getting rid of the shit-stirrers, even though we didn't have replacements yet.

Don't tolerate the shit-stirrers. They will ruin your band and drive wonderful people away.

Avoid Chaos

One of my favorite sayings is "generality creates chaos." Here's what I mean: if a band member comes to me and says, "This girl is terrible! She never learns any of her tunes!" my response is, "Any at all?"

Every time the answer is something like, "Well, most of them."

So then I walk them through each song and ask which ones the singer doesn't know. By the end, it's only 10 percent of the tunes, and we now know what lines she needs to work on.

Generality creates chaos and resentment. By being specific, we can find and fix the real problems. And sometimes, looking at a problem objectively shows you what things you're okay to live with.

Musicians carry a big bag of nonstop complaints. They complain about each other, the sound, the lights, the monitors, everything (see? I'm doing it now). And anytime a complaint comes in, it's usually generalized and vague. You can't fix something general, and you can't defend against something vague.

The answer is to calm them down and go through the issues, like a doctor going through a checklist to find your problem. The answer could be as easy as just moving a light because someone can't see. Remove the vagueness, and you'll clean up the chaos every time.

Don't Make Decisions When You're Angry

As a band leader, you're going to get frustrated. You're going to feel, at times, like the band is out of your control. You're going to get fed up with all that complaining. And ultimately, you will have to give final warnings and even fire the shit-stirrers. But don't do it when you're angry. Don't let your frustration boil to the point where you start throwing out ultimatums. When you're emotional, you often make the wrong decisions and say hurtful things that take months to heal, if they heal at all. I'm an expert in anger, and it does not work.

One of my singers complained so much about everything under the sun that I finally said, "Lord, have mercy. Do you ever stop complaining?"

She looked me straight in the eyes and said, "Well, the squeaky wheel gets the oil."

"That is true a couple of times, and if it keeps on squeaking, you change the fucking wheel." She got the point, and we had a great laugh, but I could have responded differently, especially if the issue was something like missing rehearsals, which I cannot stand. I could have thrown my weight around and said something like "We have three rehearsals a week. If you miss one more rehearsal, get the hell out." That's an ultimatum. I tried that tactic, and it fired back.

Don't use threats as a means of negotiation. They damage good spirit and goodwill in your relationships and can ultimately lead to burned bridges and lost friendships.

If you have an issue with a band member, understand that the member himself isn't the problem. The problem is rooted in an action that's being taken (or not taken) according to your brand promise or your values, and there is a solution.

Maybe your keyboard player doesn't want to rehearse three nights a week because he feels that he already knows his tunes. If you threaten him, he may leave, and you're going to spend the time you would have been rehearsing looking for a new keyboardist.

At the same time, don't make exceptions. Keyboardists, and every other musician, need to be at rehearsals like everyone else. None of this "Oh, I understand. Why don't you stay at home while we all work for the next three hours." Most of the time their excuses are just that—excuses. If they happen to be legit, you can suggest that they assist with the sound, or play the chords and assist with the harmonies, or practice the groove with the band to make it sit and feel great, or maybe work on presentation. I have never met a musician who couldn't improve something even if they know their parts inside out. But whatever you do, don't make an exception. They have to stay at rehearsal like everyone else.

No matter what happens, don't make rash decisions. Rather than give ultimatums or compromise, wait until you calm down and can find the happy medium. Look for a solution that maintains your relationships and your business's integrity.

YOUR ART NEEDS STRUCTURE

To function properly and achieve your dreams, your art needs structure. Without it, you have pure chaos, and you'll never make any real money from your music. If you're not treating your band like a business, you're robbing yourself of an amazing opportunity.

Embrace the business structure. Manage your people. Be the jockey and take control of the wild horse that is your business. Doing so will ensure you take it far into the future.

IDENTIFY THE STRUCTURE

Right off the top of your head, write down the answers to the following questions:

- Who would you love to work with?
- Who pisses you off and why?
- What repertoire will you play?
- How will the band dress onstage?
- What will you promise and deliver to the bar owner that is 30 to 100 percent better than the next band?
- What will you offer the musicians that is 30 to 100 percent better than the last band leader?

Your band is a business, and you need to start thinking about every aspect of the structure. You may think that offering more money is what musicians want. Even though that may be true sometimes, often what they really want and value most is structure, vision, and proper execution of both.

Write a story of who you'd love to work with, post it on social media, and tag me with #thebandisabusiness #gigforlife.

PARTNERS

BOOK A GIG

n the 1960s and '70s, Montreal was the Mecca of music in Canada, partly because many Americans dodged the draft by moving to Canada, among them top musicians, which gave the music scene in Montreal a very hip vibe. Various ethnic groups mixed with the French culture that appreciated art and music in all of its forms: Lower Bishop Street was home to the classic rock gigs, Crescent Street had all the discos and dance clubs, Saint Denis had the rock and blues, Saint Laurent had the funk, and Old Montreal had the jazz and fusion. Montreal is still home to the Montreal Jazz Festival, the world's largest jazz festival.

As mentioned, our band, According to Roger, eventually became a regular at Nuit Magique, which later became a classic R & B joint in Old Montreal, but in the early days, we took what we could get. When we had been together for around four months, our agent booked our first real gig in a shithole bar in a small town called Pine Hill. We should have thought twice about playing in a town that ends in "hill"—the same goes for "ville"—but it was a gig, and we were young and ready to roll.

Still, I had my eyes on something greater—Deja Vu. It was a small club on Bishop Street, but from my perspective, its popularity made it seem like Carnegie Hall.

One day, Mike, Roger, and I were driving to rehearsal. Roger was behind the wheel, deep in thought, and I sat in the passenger seat next to him. Suddenly, I turned around and said to Mike in the back seat, "I'm firing our fucking agent."

"What?!" Mike said.

"He's not giving me the gigs I want. I want to play Deja Vu. You told me that was *the* place to play, right?"

"Yeah."

"Well, that's where I want to play."

"Come on, man. I'm from Montreal, and I've heard about this place for as long as I can remember. You can't just get Deja Vu. We're nobodies. We don't have the experience. It takes years on the circuit before you can play there."

I slammed my hand down on the dashboard, startling Roger.

"Mike, we are going to get fucking Deja Vu," I screamed. "It's just a damn bar. We can do whatever we want, man.

Fuck the agent, and fuck all those other bands. We are going to get Deja Vu, period!"

Mike looked at me like I had lost my mind. "Georges, calm down, man. We have to be reasonable."

Roger looked at me with a naughty little grin, stared straight ahead, and then looked back at me, but he never said a word. That was the first time he tasted my colorful Lebanese nature.

Within a week, I walked into Deja Vu and asked for a gig. The answer was a flat no because our band was a complete unknown.

Unfazed, I asked, "Okay, who is your most popular band?"

The owner sighed and said, "Dr. Sax."

"Dr. Sax, huh?" I said and then turned around and left. Dr. Sax's band was popular mainly because of Orville, the doctor himself. He had that rare ability to play and sing, and he moved like Junior Walker.

I was not famous for thinking shit through, and no one has ever complimented me on my patience. I immediately called the doctor.

"Hey, man," I said when he answered. "You want to do a gig at Deja Vu? My singer can't make it." This, of course, was not true. Janis was just fine.

"Who are you?" Dr. Sax asked.

"My name is Georges, but never mind that, man. Can you do the gig?"

"Yo yo yo, I own that gig, man. That's my joint. I don't need anyone to book me there."

"I dig that, but your band can't play there every week. We need a front person, and we play a very similar repertoire. You interested?"

"How much you paying?"

"How much money do you want?"

I can't remember the exact number, but it was a stupidly high amount, as much as most musicians made in three days.

I paused, knowing he was full of shit, and then said, "Sure, you're on." He probably thought I was naive as hell.

At that point, I didn't actually have the gig booked, so I walked back to Deja Vu and told the owner, "I have a band."

"Who's your front person?" No one cares who the drummer is, which was me. The first thing the club owner wants to know is who's up front.

"Dr. Sax."

"Dr. Sax?" The owner was dumbfounded.

"Yeah, man. He wants to do this gig with us. We have a great repertoire."

"Dr. Sax?"

"Yeah, Dr. Sax."

End of conversation, because Dr. Sax was this guy's best act.

A lot of people get stuck on money, which is funny for a group of people who hate the word *business*. I got zero dollars for that gig because I basically gave everything we made to Dr. Sax, but it was worth it. His clout got me access.

Before you can go anywhere in this business, you have to book a gig, and then another, and then another. This chapter will show you how.

DO YOUR RESEARCH

As mentioned in Track 2, it's easy to get overwhelmed by big tasks like "book a gig." Like everything else on this journey, break it down into smaller steps and then keep asking yourself, *What's next?* To book a gig, you need to start with research on each venue, its customers, and its owner.

Let's say someone gives you a tip that a certain bar is hiring. Then you find out that it's a smooth jazz club, and you have a rock band. First, you'll have to find out whether the owner even hires rock bands. You'll also have to learn how many musicians they can afford and whether that changes based on the night you play. Some bars hire a five-piece band on the weekends and only two-piece bands on Monday and Tuesday when customer volume is low.

DON'T BE SALESY

New musicians tell bar owners their band's story with all the passion in the world, and owners get excited by the band's excitement. But if your band is not ready, you just lost a connection. Musicians sometimes think that if they sell their band one time, they're in for life. How are you going to get the second gig with a terrible sound?

If there's one thing that bar owners hate, it's being sold to. Salesy is not very far from sleazy. Don't be so salesy. Show your true value. Deliver on your promise.

You may be thinking, But, Georges, how can I deliver if they won't let me in? How can I get in without selling?

To me, the fastest way in is through referrals or recommendations from musicians you've played with. If someone comes to a club owner and says, "I played with James Brown," that means something because, well, do you think James Brown would play with a flake?

Getting and keeping the gig has nothing to do with your suit, your skirt, your makeup, or your tight abs. It has everything to do with delivering on your promise. People can't argue with numbers. If you can say, "When my band plays, sales go up 30 percent—I've played with this other band, and they can vouch for me," people will take notice.

Visit the bar to get a feel for the overall vibe. Find out what kind of customers go there, what they wear, what gets them excited, what songs they react to and which ones are duds. If it's a country and western club, you can expect to see blue jeans, pearl snaps, and boots, but still go check out the crowd. The same goes for a bar that plays mainly rock or funk. Once you see how the audience shows up, you'll know how to dress to match the vibe, and then take it up a notch.

Talk to the band that's performing the night you visit. Find out what it's like to play there and what the owner's expectations are. What does he love? What drives him absolutely crazy? If the top item on his "hate" list is the music your band plays or if he doesn't allow dancing and your sets are designed to get people on their feet, that club might not be the one for you.

LIVE ENTERTAINMENT VENUES

One thing to keep in mind is that live entertainment venues can last twenty, thirty, even forty years. They far outlast discos and venues that rely on DJs and fancy lights and the latest smoke machine. That means it is well worth your time and energy to build those relationships with bar owners, because if you do, you could have a gig for life in no time.

MAKE YOUR FAVORS COUNT

You're going to need a lot of favors, especially when you first start, so use them wisely. Don't be annoying. Don't ask for little things you could really do yourself. If you repeatedly ask for small things, you won't have any "tokens" left when it comes time for the big asks.

Also, make the favors count when you are on the receiving end. They can be used as leverage. If the bar owner asks you to do two more songs or even an extra set, you could say, "Bro, it's my pleasure. Happy to do it. But let me go to the guys with something in return. It's been a pain point for them to do that one-hour set at the end of the night. Can I tell them that from now on, it will be forty minutes like all the other sets?"

GET TO KNOW YOUR VENUE PARTNERS

If all your research tells you that the venue is a good fit and you decide to book the gig, you need to do a little more learning up front. The two biggest parts of the venue ecosystem are the bar owner and the staff. If you want to book more than one gig at this place, you need to get to know the people you'll be working with, set boundaries, and establish a positive relationship from the beginning.

First, you'll want to set up a meeting with the owner to get detailed answers to a ton of questions:

- *Where should we park for the gig? Where should we park for the soundcheck?* You definitely don't want to park in the customer spots or the owner's precious reserved space.

- *When* exactly *is soundcheck?* Let them know that you'll need two hours at full volume to get the proper sound. You don't want to just show up and have no staff there to let you in, and you also don't want to prep for the gig in the middle of happy hour.

- *Do you have any songs or genres you'd like us to avoid?* Sometimes another band will have just played a certain song, and they're tired of it. Or an owner may want to attract a certain crowd with a certain genre and repertoire.

- *What kind of volume do you prefer?* If they want dancing, let them know it requires a minimum volume. Nobody dances to a whisper. It's a live show, and there's no excitement without volume.

- *Do you want us to interact with the crowd?* Some like you to be playful, and others just want the music without the theatrics.

- *Do you want the band sitting with customers? If so, for how long?* This will often depend on if you're freeloading. The bar owner may want you to mingle to a point or not at all.

- *Do you want your customers to dance?* Some owners don't want to encourage dancing because they believe if people are dancing they're not drinking. Others want you to pack the dance floor.

- *Which bartender do we order from?* You don't want six bartenders serving the band and not the crowd. Get one guy to take all your orders and talk to one bartender. No one ever asks this to bar owners.

- *What area of the bar would you like us to sit in?* I never allow my bands to sit at the main bar. That is very precious real estate for the bar. Instead, ask the owner which table you can use.

- *Do you give the band free drinks or at least a discount?* I always negotiate free drinks for the band before the gig is booked, one per set.

- *Do you want encores?* Encores can show people that the bar hires good bands. But sometimes the staff will be pissed off for having to work longer.

- *Would you like us to hang around after the gig?* Some owners like the extra drink sales from your band, and others want you to finish and leave.

Though you should definitely ask these questions before your first gig, don't ask that one time only. Check in again and again. Bar owners change and adjust their practices, but they won't always think to tell you.

In addition, I recommend making certain requests of the bar owner before you ever step on his stage:

- *Talk to* me *if you have a problem with anyone in the band.* I don't let bar owners express anger to any of my musicians. Musicians are emotional people and play from their hearts. It's extremely difficult to take shit from bar owners and then get back up onstage to entertain *their* customers. It's important that you don't fuck with the vibe. I know how and when to talk to my guys.

- *Let me know who your point person is.* Just as you want the bar owner to come to you only, find out the one person you should go to on behalf of the band. Having a single point of contact will keep communication smooth and eliminate any irritants.

- *Ask your staff to go through your point person.* Every waitress and bartender thinks they're the owner. You don't want some waitress standing in the middle of the dance floor gesturing to turn the volume down in the middle of your set. They should go through the bar owner's point person, who should come talk directly to you—and not in the middle of a set.

When I talk to the bar owner and the contact person, I make sure I'm friendly and respectful, because I expect the same from them. Band members are not second-class citizens. The point person should not make them feel like she's doing them a favor every time she gets them a drink. If she does, talk to the owner.

Also, get to know the bartender, servers, and staff, because many times, if the staff doesn't like you, you're not coming back. Find out what the staff members are like. Find out whether one of the waiters is the owner's boyfriend. Find out if they complain about hearing the same tunes night after night.

The staff members are a funky part of the ecosystem. You can be an amazing band that packs the house every night and makes the owner a lot of money, but the staff may still hate you—sometimes for the very reasons that the others love you. They may hate you *because* of how successful you are. They may be resentful (and jealous!) because they think musicians are just a bunch of flakes who sleep till noon, work for three hours, get free drinks, get applause, and then go home with the hottest guy or girl in the bar. They can come to work each night with a "Who the hell do you think you are?" or "They don't have real jobs, and I'm busting my ass" type of attitude. And sometimes for good reason—the stereotypical prima donna musician didn't come out of nowhere. Many waitresses and bartenders have been disrespected by musicians who think very highly of themselves and look down on the staff.

You and your band will have to break through these predetermined beliefs, and you need a strategy to do it right. You have to go out of your way to make the staff realize that you're all in this together. Let them know you appreciate their hard work, that you're a team serving the customers. Ask them how their day was. Thank them from the microphone. Basically, let them know they are *valuable*. Make the same effort with the staff as you do with the audience and club owner.

Even if you do all of that, you may still have some tough characters to deal with on the staff. Some people are simply a pain in the ass. Still, you have to find a way to work with them. You and your band might be tempted to react with a "Yeah? Well screw you too!" attitude. I understand. It's difficult to get the same negative vibe every night and just smile. But that attitude is not the way to win over the staff. You need to kill them with kindness. Don't let them turn you into what they are. If you do, you'll start discriminating. You'll start treating certain people better than others. You'll begin smiling at these people and not at those. It's just a matter of time before you're never smiling. Then you'll just become a walking grouch, and what bar is going to book and rebook that kind of energy? Plus, think about it this way: if you can handle those types of people with a smile, you can handle anyone.

Be centered. Tell yourself to kill them with kindness. Walk up to that waitress and ask her how her day was or how her sick child is, even though you know she wants to rip the eyes out of your head.

If you neglect one element at your gig, such as your relationship with the staff, then the entire experience at that bar is null. Be aware and provide an atmosphere of love, joy, and respect on all fronts. This will make people want to work with you. Meaning, they'll pay you 30 percent more than the next guy, and you'll have gigs booked for months.

THINK LIKE THE BAR OWNER

The bar owners' prime objective in hiring musicians is to make money. Period. They don't care about what they see as the fluffy shit like "Oh, music is wonderful, and it lifts people's souls." They aren't in the business of promoting bands like yours. They are in the business of entertaining people and selling drinks.

That doesn't mean bar owners aren't passionate about music. People who open a live music venue usually love live music. They love inviting people to their bar to have a drink and listen to the band. It gives them a sense of prestige.

But at the end of the day, the bar owner is thinking, *Man, I got to pay rent.* He's wondering, *If I hire you, will I make money? Will my customers get excited and tell their friends about how wonderful you are?* No matter how much they love music, owners need to sell drinks to make money. If they don't sell drinks, their business is gone—and so is your gig.

Keep that in mind when you talk to bar owners. Put yourself in their shoes. They aren't your enemy. They aren't trying to take advantage of you. They are trying to make money and further their business just like you.

I've heard musicians say things like, "This is bullshit, man. They pay us fifty bucks, but they're making so much money. They keep all the real money for themselves and take advantage of us."

My answer to this line of thinking is this: "If bar owners are such pricks, why are they all bankrupt?"

If bar ownership was really profitable and all these guys had to do was take advantage of musicians to make money, there'd be thousands of bars around. If you think of bar owners as enemies, you'll never create a partnership that will be mutually beneficial to you and them. Remember: this business isn't all about you. It's about you and your partners marrying your goals so you all win. Don't walk into the bar and tell the owner how great you are. Tell him how your presence is beneficial to his goals.

When customers are happy, they stay an extra hour and buy another drink. When customers are happy, they come back another time during the week instead of Fridays only. When that happens, the bar makes more money. If you can help bar owners make more money, you're the greatest band that ever walked the planet Earth. That's how you book the gig again and again.

And that's really your goal. You don't want to go into the bar and do one weekend gig. What's the point? If you've put all that work into booking the gig, meeting with the bar owner, rehearsing, and so on, you want to get as much mileage as possible from it. If you don't, you might as well do a one-off event like a wedding or play music for fun and not try to have a career in the industry at all. But if you want to gig for life, you need relationships with six or seven bars that hire you on a regular basis. (More on rebooking later in this track.) If you can think like a bar owner from the beginning, you'll have a career in music from the start, as well as for years to come.

GET IT IN WRITING

Let's say you booked your first gig. You've established yourself through referrals and recommendations from people the bar owner trusts, and the owner hired you for a Thursday night. What happens now?

Find out exactly what the bar owner expects the night of your gig, and get it in writing. How formal that piece of writing is depends on the type of gig. If you're playing at a wedding, some corporate event, or a hotel gig, get a contract. But, if you are playing at your local bar on Wednesday night, a text message that lays out the specifics is sufficient. Don't ask your local club owner for a contract. If they want you to sign one, do it, but in my experience, a simple email or message is all that's needed with these venues.

Sometimes bar owners are looking for something really specific, but they don't know how to articulate their desires. Or they assume you know what needs to be done, or they rattle the steps off so quickly, it's easy to lose track of what's important in the conversation. Communication with the bar owner is usually verbal, but verbal communication is exactly that, words: they're spoken and then they're gone. You have to get it in writing. If it's not written, it doesn't exist.

Nowadays, this is pretty easy to do. For example, immediately after your conversation, send the owner a text: "I just want to make sure I understand you, so I can serve you better. Three sets, the first two are 40 minutes, the last one is 30. Sound check at 6 p.m. $800/night. Is this what you meant?"

Something as simple as this means you have a written record of what you agreed on. It's something to fall back on if a disagreement arises. It's hard for someone to argue with an email or text that clearly states what they've agreed to.

When you do get the gig specifics in writing, contract or otherwise, you'll need to make sure a few items are mentioned. For example:

- How much does the gig pay?
- When is the gig?
- How many nights do you play for?
- How many sets do you play a night?
- When are you expected to pick up your equipment? The day after or as soon as you're done?
- How will you be paid? Ten days later or on the spot?
- Will you be paid with cash? Wire? Check?
- If you're paid with a check, how do you know that it won't bounce?
- How long are the sets? How long are the breaks?
- Do you get free drinks?
- Do you bring your own sound equipment, or is it provided?

You should also add whatever is a deal-breaker for you— the one thing you won't budge on. It could be more money or a certain number of gigs or free drinks for your guys. Make sure it's all in writing.

FIRST SIGNED, FIRST SERVED

If you accept a gig and sign a contract—even if it's an email or text stating your agreement—you need to keep that commitment, even if a different bar suddenly offers you four times as much for the same night. The first bar that makes the agreement is the first bar served, no exceptions. You keep this principle, and you will be known as a band that keeps their word no matter what.

NEGOTIATE

Negotiation is part of life. I have to negotiate with my son to get him to sleep at night, and then I have to negotiate with him to get up in the morning. I have to negotiate with him to do his homework. All day long, all I do is negotiate.

If you don't know how to negotiate, you're going to have a tough time—not just in business, but in life too.

My trick for negotiating is this: I ask myself, *What is the one thing that means everything to me?* Then I focus on getting that one thing.

Let's say when I sent a bar owner a contract, he came back and said, "No, no, we don't want to do this. Change it to this, this, and this." I look at the deal I thought we were making and ask myself, *What is the one thing I'm not willing to budge on?* There are some things that mean nothing to me. I don't give a shit if the sound check is at seven o'clock instead of six. But I do care if the bar owner said we'd have the weekend spot and now we're getting the week-front. Or if he said we'd get a thousand dollars a night, but now he's saying it's seven hundred.

I also make sure to word my requests as suggestions or questions, rather than demands. For example, use words like, "I was thinking...," "How about...," "Would it be okay if...," "Is this reasonable to you...," "In my experience, I have found that...," and "I want to run this by you..."

It's easier to negotiate if you've already proven yourself with this bar owner and you've established a relationship. Still, even if this is your first gig in a certain place, you can't let people walk all over you. Be respectful and kill them with kindness, but hold your ground on what's important to you.

What is your one thing? Many people think it's the money, but for me it's making sure my band gets free drinks. I may let go of a hundred dollars in salary and keep my band happy, so they don't waste their paycheck on booze and go home with nothing in their pocket and feel discouraged.

If I'm trying to break into a new venue or a new town, my one thing might be that I want a Saturday night gig, and not Thursday. If a bar has two locations in the city and my one thing is to play in both so my band has consistent income, I might negotiate like this: "Okay, I understand you don't want to pay me X. How about this: I will make you a deal for the first four gigs. If I am not fired by the fifth, you will then have to pay me X and book me in both bars for at least ten weekends this year."

Bottom line: hang on to your one thing, your deal breaker, and be flexible on the other stuff.

You might even ask the bar owner or the manager what their one thing is, but you need to be careful with how you ask. If one of your band members wants to date the staff you can't just walk up and say, "Hey, can we date your bartender?"

Sometimes you need to be like a psychologist and ask questions around the question. Ask them about their worst experience with another band. Ask what annoys their regulars. Ask what they wish would never happen again. If you listen closely, you'll find out what the owner's one thing is, and then make sure you take that into account during your negotiations. You'll know what things you shouldn't push too much and what things to stay away from completely.

You can save yourself a lot of time and heartache by having a conversation with the owner about his deal-breakers before you ever play there. For me, a deal-breaker is that we get paid the minute we finish, not two days later. If your one thing doesn't line up with the bar owner's—for example, if he usually does pay two days later—it may be better to not play there. But if they do line up—boom! Everybody wins, and you'll have a lifetime relationship, which is the goal, after all.

One thing to keep in mind: negotiation is not a competition. It's a way to make sure both parties get what they need. It's easy to forget that on the other side of the table is a human being who has a life. They have children, a wife, a dog, and hobbies. They have emotions, thoughts, judgments, and opinions that are all developing in real time as you sit at the table together. Taking an extra few minutes at the beginning of a conversation to get to know them is a well-spent investment. Your friendliness, your approach, the way you say things, and your posture all affect the bar owner's opinion of you. And in the end, it's his opinion that gets you the gig.

One of the best ways I've learned to sway someone's opinion during negotiating is to have a great sense of humor. I once had a meeting with a major hotel, and they invited me to meet in their office. I normally meet on neutral ground, like the hotel coffee shop, but they insisted this time. When I arrived, I found myself greeted by the entire management team: the GM, director of food and beverage, the director of finance, everyone, and as usual they were all dressed in suits and ties.

The first thing I said when I walked in and looked around was, "You brought the whole team? I'm shaking from fear! How the hell am I going to defend myself against all this intellectual power?"

The tension broke, and they started laughing. I said, "Screw you guys. You know me well. You can bring the whole world in here, and I'm still going to be me." We had a big laugh and then started the meeting in a friendly tone and a relaxed atmosphere, which ended in a win-win. (It should be noted that you have to know your relationship in each interaction. I was able to joke like this because I already had a great relationship.)

I still use this tactic today. If I get the feeling that somebody wants to start pushing me around at a meeting, I call it out and start acting like a kid saying, "Ow! Ow! Come on man, stop beating me!" and we laugh. You have to know when to break the tension.

This works with dealing with bands and in your personal life too. Never lose your inner child. In the end, you are dealing with human beings who just want to have fun, even during negotiations. Don't take yourself so seriously.

Also, don't use ultimatums when you're negotiating. Be kind, smile, talk very little, and listen a lot. Nod your head. Say, "I see" and "I understand." Those phrases work whether you agree or disagree. So does, "I've never thought about it that way."

Another good strategy when negotiating contracts is to group all the things you agree with first. That way during the negotiation, you can immediately go down the list and say, "My pleasure" and "No problem." Then, at the *very* end, after you've been so agreeable for so long, you bring up the *one* thing that you disagree with. They almost have to agree to it. Otherwise, they will feel awkward because it's clear there is no give and take and that they are not willing to come your way a little even though you have agreed to so many of their requirements.

That's the beauty of this strategy. You come into a negotiation fully informed. You're charming, playful, making them feel comfortable, being completely agreeable, and making them like you. Now you can ask for whatever you want. I highly recommend reading Dale Carnegie's book *How to Win Friends and Influence People*.

Being open makes for better communication as well. If you and I spend time getting to know each other and I say something that may seem unreasonable or offensive, you'll know that I didn't mean it like that. You'll know who I am and what I really meant. This is another reason I always prefer meeting face to face or with a video call at a minimum. I want to see the other person smile and know that they don't think I'm being difficult. Everything is exposed. No hiding for either party.

BUILD TRUST

If Dr. Sax walks into a club and says, "I want $300 a night," bar owners will immediately agree because they know he packs the place.

If a new musician hears how much Dr. Sax makes, he might try the same thing. Doing this is like googling the salary of an engineer, seeing that it's between $80,000 and $300,000, and saying at your first job interview after graduation, "I want to make $300,000." The hiring manager would look at you like, *Who the hell does this guy think he is?*

You can't walk into a bar and start rattling off what you want. It's not your bar. It's like you walking in my house saying, "I don't like the couch here. I want to move it there." It's not your house. We have to get to know each other a *lot* better before you can start telling me where to put my couch.

Before you start making demands, give bar owners the meat and potatoes. Deliver on your brand promise. Bring in the customers. Once you've proven that you can serve them what they want to be served, you'll have more room to do your thing. Once you've established trust, then you can make a recommendation. Eventually, the owners will welcome your remarks and say, "You know what? That's a great idea, man."

Remember: don't make recommendations based on what's good for you. Make them based on what's best for the bar. The owners have seen hundreds of musicians—they can tell if you're trying to genuinely help them.

THE BOSS IS ALWAYS THE BOSS

After you play in the same venue for a while, you will probably become friends with the manager. You might even socialize outside of the venue. If that happens, remember this: the boss is always the boss.

If you go out with them and get drunk or smoke up or just let loose, you all may be having fun that night, but the next day, that manager or owner will remember what you did and said—even if they were part of it. After that, they may judge you and stop trusting you and even avoid working with you again.

They will also remember if you started asking for favors or tried to slip in a sales pitch. Don't insult their intelligence. Stay respectful and alert or you might find yourself out of a gig.

Another part of building trust is knowing your value. In the 1985 Sting documentary *Bring on the Night*, Sting's manager, Miles Copeland, tells a story about a meeting that took place with Sting's musicians about money negotiations. One of them asks, "How much money is on the table, man?"

Copeland looks at him and says, "It's not your table. It's Sting's table. If one of you guys doesn't show up and we get a replacement, every single person would still show up. If Sting doesn't show up, how many people would return their tickets? Every single one of them."

Those musicians were some of the best in the world, but they still didn't have the value that Sting has.

If your band was supposed to play the third week of October and for some reason you couldn't make it and another band took over, would your absence affect the bar's revenue that night? If the answer is yes, then you have value to that bar owner and you're now in a better position to ask for more money. But if the answer is no, then you have to consider whether you're really bringing the value that you promised. Are you really worth what they're paying you now? The principle is simple: create more value, ask for more money.

STAY IN YOUR CIRCLE OF INFLUENCE

If you get a gig that ends up not going 100 percent smoothly, don't start blaming everyone and everything else. Don't blame the lighting, the sound system, the bad bar service, the fact that the bar didn't do marketing—basically, don't blame all of the factors you can't control.

You were hired to play guitar, sing songs, and entertain the crowd. That's it. That's what you can control. If you did your homework up front and talked to other bands, you should have known about the lighting, the sound system, and the bad service. If you signed a contract knowing all of those things, then stop all the unproductive nonsense. Don't try to fix the bar or point out all of the things they should be doing. That's not your job. Focus on what you actually can control. Besides, whining will likely get you fired.

REBOOK

Once a gig is booked, there is no guarantee that you'll be booked again. Anyone can be impressed with posters and videos and doing an amazing job on a Saturday night. But if you do something stupid on any other day, I guarantee that you'll never go back.

Rebooking is more important than the initial booking. This is actually the ultimate goal of all the research and relationship building and negotiating. It's all part of proving yourself as a professional and building trust with the owner so that you can start booking gigs for years at a time.

When I was still playing and leading the band, I would approach the bar owner once we had proven our worth and built trust. "Look, I'm having to chase you down every week. I don't have time for this. You don't have time for this. Let's help each other." Then I'd ask, "Are you happy with the band? Do you trust what I do?"

They would always say yes because I had proven myself as a professional and had already been getting repeat bookings. So then I'd say, "Okay. Give me eight weeks. You're giving them to me anyway. Let's just save each other the time and book them all now so that you don't have to think about it." I always present this idea as a service I'm doing for them, but the reality is, it helps both of us.

Many bar owners are afraid of that commitment. If they hesitated when I proposed booking eight weeks, I'd say, "No problem. Let's just get something solid in the books, and you can cancel any time. Feel better?" And they'd feel even better if we put that in writing. The point is *just get the gigs booked.*

The truth is, you really are helping the bar owner by booking several months in advance. It's draining for them to deal with making sure they have a band every weekend. You're taking another burden off their shoulders. What bar owner wouldn't agree to you saying, "I want to free you from all that back-and-forth nonsense. Let's book it all now, and I'll just show up on that day"?

On your side, it's also a huge plus for keeping the band together. Musicians feel secure when you tell them that you already have gigs set up for the next year. They'll stick with you even if somebody offers them higher pay. This exact model has worked for me for the last thirty-plus years over an enormous volume of shows and hundreds of musicians. And don't worry about missing out on other gigs because you're all booked up. You might miss a wedding here or there, but the trade-off is having a year's worth of gigs lined up. Remember: it's not the one gig that pays great that you should prioritize. It's how much money you made at the end of the year.

How fast this happens depends on how fast the trust is built. It could take two gigs for some bands and four for another. But whenever you sense that they trust you, that's when you go up to the owner and say, "You know, I was thinking we could help each other..." Any club owner in his right mind wouldn't turn that down. You get to keep your band booked, and he gets to quit worrying about all the scheduling. Win-win.

If you can get six bars to agree to eight weeks of gigs, boom—you've booked the next eleven to twelve months. This is the most efficient way to have a gig for life.

DON'T WAIT, BOOK NOW

One of the biggest mistakes musicians make is saying, "Next time." They're at a bar, and the vibe is right. They had a good talk with the owner about their band. But they don't take the next step to talk specifics. "Next time," they say.

Timing is everything. You have to kiss the girl when the candles are lit and strike the iron while it's hot. Book the gig *now*, while the owner still remembers who you are.

Before you leave, ask the owner what dates he has available and book one. There are a lot more musicians than there are bars, so calendars fill up fast. As you build trust and prove your value, try to book more than one, but for now, get one on the calendar and start preparing.

The next track will help you get ready for that first gig, and all those that follow.

CHALLENGE

NEGOTIATE THE ONE THING

Write down everything the gig entails: the money that you want, the number of nights you'll play, if it's a five or four-piece band, whether you'll address the audience, the number of gigs in a row, the number of sets a night. Then circle the one thing that you won't budge on. Approach the negotiation with the bar owner with that in mind. Just work with the owner to try to get everything he wants while protecting your "one thing."

Write a story of how you negotiated the gig, or just write "I got the gig," and tag me with #bookagig #gigforlife.

PREPARE FOR YOUR GIG

n 1997, my band Elchakieh had an opportunity to audition for a gig in Hong Kong. Gigs in Montreal were a lot different from those in Asia. Canadians did not have high expectations from entertainment, whereas Asians put a big emphasis on dancing, choreography, and other visual aspects of the show. So when it came time to record our audition video, we got help from a gentleman named Curtis Patterson, who represented the agency in Asia. He had played the kind of music we would be playing and knew what the audiences expected.

I was excited to try this new choreographed style, but my band didn't share my enthusiasm. I heard things like, "To hell with that, man. We just want to sing," and "I can't dance, man. I have two left feet. Plus, how am I supposed to dance with my wire and mic stand in the way?

We had a lot of debates, but they agreed to give it a shot. When Curtis came to one of our practices where we were working on choreography and dancing, he made us try it again and again and again, shouting out different instructions: "Lift your shoulders." "Don't do that thing with your head." "When he's playing this, you do that."

When Curtis saw how frustrated we were getting, he told us a story. "One time, I was in Japan with this band. We were really good, but the crowd just didn't react. Our whole band left the stage thinking we'd done a great job. We didn't even notice that the crowd wasn't engaged.

"After we went to the dressing room, the Japanese bar owner walked in and closed the door. He looked up at us standing around him, raised his hand high above his head, and shook his finger in our faces while he yelled, 'Rehearth! Rehearth! Rehearth!' and then turned around and walked out. The message was clear: our performance was messy. We needed to improve or risk getting fired."

My band got the message, too, when Curtis told that story: don't underestimate the power in the details of every aspect of your performances. The way you hold your head, how you move to the music, how loud you sing, your intros and outros—it all needs to be practiced. Your partners, the bar or nightclub owners, have taken a risk by hiring you to play. Now you need to make sure you deliver so that you all reap the benefits. The only way to do that is to rehearse, rehearse, rehearse.

In this track, we'll divide the parts of your gig into two main sections: musical mechanics and visual presentation onstage. Both need to be practiced in detail before you ever take the stage.

FIX IT IN THE FACTORY

Eighty percent of any gig is mechanics, and rehearsals are the factory in which you build the amazing machine that you bring out onstage. The more fine-tuned your assembly line behind the scenes becomes, the more chance you have to shine in public and achieve your goals, as well as the venue owners' goals. Whatever happens onstage is a direct result of what happens during rehearsals.

Many musicians lack this understanding. They don't realize that the rehearsal *is* the show, that whatever attitude they bring to rehearsals is the attitude they will bring onstage. So they approach rehearsals in a distracted, half-ass way, saying, "I'm tired, man. Don't worry. I'll put more energy into the show onstage tonight." No, they won't. I'll say it again: the quality of each show is always a direct result of the quality of your rehearsals.

This means that you have to do the rehearsal *exactly* as you intend to perform onstage in front of an audience. I don't let my guys sit around and tell me, "I'm saving my voice" or "I'll sound better tonight" or "I'll dance at the gig."

Bullshit. You need to practice every aspect of the show in rehearsal so that you can fix what needs fixing and practice over and over again until you get it right.

When you hit the stage, it's too late to fix anything. By that time, all kinds of variables come into play: adrenaline, alcohol, harsh lighting, different sound equipment, and most importantly the crowd. With all of those distractions, your show will never be better than the rehearsal. If your skills aren't already honed, developed, and perfected, your emotions will overwhelm you. The more skilled and well-rehearsed you are, the less you will rely on your emotions while onstage, which is a good thing because emotions are unreliable. They change all the time. But when you know your shit inside out, the moves and vocals will all come out naturally no matter what your mood is.

Do you really think that those big stars slack off during rehearsals? Think again. Michael Jackson used to videotape his rehearsals and review them over and over again. He knew exactly what was going to happen onstage because he fixed the issues in practice. As a result, he delivered perfection onstage every single time, even when he was being sued and his personal life was anything but easygoing. He had practiced so much that his body didn't even need the right emotions to do its job.

As the band leader, part of your job is to make sure everyone gets it done in the rehearsal factory. You need to anticipate your band members' habits and know who has a tendency to come to rehearsal unprepared or unwilling to give 100 percent, and then take preemptive action. I learned this the hard way. I would come to rehearsal and be frustrated with the same people for the same things they did at the last rehearsal. It was like *Groundhog Day*. One day I thought, *What the hell am I doing?* and started thinking about what I could do *before* rehearsals to make it better.

I already mentioned one trick: I started having musicians who knew their lyrics and dance moves go help those who were struggling. I also started briefing the band more regularly. I sent email reminders about rehearsals and upcoming events. I made it very clear what time we were starting. If downbeat was at 3:00 p.m., they needed to gather at 2:30 to get a drink, go to the bathroom, chit-chat, tune their instruments, and debrief about the issues we needed to fix from the previous show. At 3:00, we dropped the first note, and we were off. No more messing around.

To deliver a Saturday night experience every night you perform, you have to take rehearsals just as seriously.

GO AWAY. WE'RE WORKING.

I guarantee you're going to get this request at least once while you're the band leader: "Can my _____ [friend, girlfriend, boyfriend, spouse] come to rehearsal?"

In the words of Dr. Evil, "How about no, you crazy Dutch bastard!" Rehearsals are serious business. Every band member needs to concentrate without distraction. Plus, you're trying out half-baked dance moves and new tunes during these rehearsals, which means that you'll make mistakes, and then embarrassment and insecurities are on full display. Sometimes you'll have debates and arguments, and tension can be high. Keep non-band members out of the work zone.

VISUALIZE THE EXPERIENCE

As the band leader, you need to visualize how the gig will go, from beginning to end. Whether you have previously designed the show in your head or scribbled ideas on paper, the picture of how it will go comes together before rehearsals, and then you bring it all together onstage.

If I asked you to describe the show to me, you should be able to talk me through it from beginning to end—including these elements, for example:

- How you will walk out onstage
- How you will greet the audience
- What songs you will play
- How you will transition from song to song
- How you want the audience to feel during each song (Sentimental? Pumped?)

- Where the showstoppers and memorable moments will be
- Which band members will do solos
- Whether you want people to dance or listen
- What will make them scream for encores
- How to close the show and walk offstage

Once you answer these questions, you will have a picture of the experience you want, for example, "My intention is to start slowly with people talking to each other, and then after a few songs, people will start to loosen up. By the end, everyone's hopping and dancing."

Some bar owners will have definite opinions on some of these things, and you'll have to take their wishes into consideration. For example, some owners will say things like, "Do not engage the audience. Just create a nice vibe, maybe some Ed Sheeran. My customers want to chat. They want to have a cigar and a whiskey. This isn't a 'put your hands up!' kind of place." If you're usually a "get the crowd moving" kind of band, you'll need to practice setting a different vibe.

Form

Once you know the experience you want to create, you need to write up a form that captures the structure of each tune. The form is not the same as a musical chart, where you write the actual notes and chords. The form is essentially a road map that identifies the sections so that everyone is looking at the same song breakdown: intro, verse, chorus, verse, chorus, bridge, chorus, chorus, out. This helps everyone communicate more clearly, which speeds things up during rehearsal.

Musicians get frustrated with singers because they don't know how to read music. If we're on bar thirty-seven during rehearsal, every musician knows the note, but most singers don't work like that. They know where we are in the song by what they hear: "When the keyboard player does this, I'll do that. When I hear this, I'll sing that." Everyone gets irritated because they're not speaking the same language.

The form literally puts everyone on the same page. Rather than having the singer say, "It's when I sing 'I love you,'" and the guitarist asks, "Is that the G7 chord?" they can both refer to the form and see that it's the second line of the third verse. The form gives them the ability to communicate and to conduct a smooth rehearsal, and it frees everyone to play with confidence because they all know where the bridge is and how many choruses there are. Also, when new members join the band, you can share the forms, so they know the arrangements right off the bat. Plus, you show them from the beginning that they have joined an organized band.

If you have some technical ability, using music writing software is a great way to add form to your lyrics. However, most singers and musicians don't think that way and just use pen and paper. Whatever works, as long as you can add some type of general form that can be understood by

Rock With You
Michael Jackson

1D	– 1
Lead-in	– 1
Intro	– 8
Verse 1	– 12
Pre-chorus 1	– 4
Chorus 1	– 8
Verse 2	– 12
Pre-chorus 2	– 4
Chorus 2	– 8
Bridge	– 8
Solo	– 16
Chorus 3&4 (Key Change)	– 16
Outro	– 8
Ending	– 1

Figure 6.1. Form Created by Hand

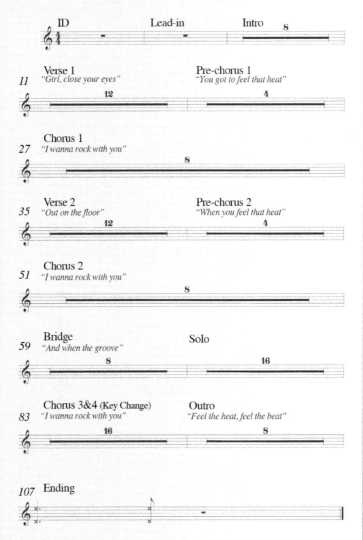

Figure 6.2. Form Created by Software

all—though I do recommend digital because it can be easily saved and shared.

Figure 6.1 shows you what it might look like if drawn by hand, and Figure 6.2 shows a form produced by software.

Lyrics

At the start of my career leading bands, I'd require every member to bring their own lyrics sheets to rehearsal to use as a reference point. The problem was that one guy would get lyrics from this website, which was slightly different from that website; another would write them down with a pencil and miss some words or misread his own writing. Eventually we agreed on one site and printed out the lyrics from there. The lyrics weren't always perfect, but at least we now all had the same lyrics, and we could correct the mistakes together in exactly the same way. Make sure everyone is looking at the same words.

For us, everything was written out; if a line started at verse one, eighth bar, then I wrote "intro eight" beside the lyric. See Figure 6.3 for a sample lyrics sheet.

Ideally, singers will look at the form along with the lyrics sheet, but many don't. They only care about the words. By marking up the lyrics, you can make sure that singers can still see the form of the song even if they don't look at the form sheet itself. They can see that when they finish singing the chorus, they need to wait sixteen bars for the guitar solo, for example, and not come in too early with the third chorus.

Rock With You
Michael Jackson

ID - 1

Lead-in - 1

Intro - 8

Verse 1 - 12

Girl, close your eyes, Let that rhythm get into you
Don't try to fight it, There ain't nothing that you can do
Relax your mind, Lay back and groove with mine

Pre-chorus 1 - 4

You gotta **feel that heat,** And we can ride the boogie
Share that beat of love

Chorus 1 - 8

I wanna rock with you **all night**
Dance you into day **sunlight**
I wanna rock with you **all night**
We gonna **rock the** night away

Verse 2 - 12

Out on the floor, There ain't nobody there but us
Girl, when you dance, There's a magic that must be love
Just take it slow, we got so far to go

(1/2)

Figure 6.3a. Sample Lyrics Sheet

Pre-chorus 2 - 4

When you *feel that heat,* And we gonna ride boogie
Share that beat of love

Chorus 2 - 8

I wanna rock with you *all night*
Dance you into day *sunlight*
I wanna rock with you *all night*
We gonna *rock the* night away

Bridge - 8

And when the groove is dead and gone yeah
You know that *love survives*, So we can *rock forever, on*

Solo - 16

I wanna rock with you, I wanna groove with you

Chorus 3&4 - 16 (Key Change)

I wanna rock with you *all night*
Dance you into day *sunlight*
I wanna rock with you *all night*
We gonna *rock the* night away

Outro - 8

Feel the heat, feel the beat *all night*
Rock you into day *sunlight*
Rock *all night*
Rock the night away

Ending - 1

Like the form, the lyrics sheet isn't just a cheat sheet for the singers. And it's more of a way to bridge the gap of communication between singers and musicians. Also, when you see it in writing, you remember the form of the tune quicker and retain it for a long time. Most musicians and singers are great at feeling the structure of a song while in the moment, but are not so great at verbalizing or expressing it explicitly. Because of this, they quickly forget how a song goes and have trouble explaining which part they're referring to. Lyrics sheets can solve this problem, so everyone knows the words and notes. In Track 7, you'll see how important it is for musicians to know the lyrics too.

EVERYONE HAS ROOM TO IMPROVE

Many great musicians think that because they can play their instrument to a very high level, they have nothing to learn before or during rehearsals. They figure, "I know what I'm doing. I can wing it," so they don't take time to learn their tunes. As a friend of mine always says, "The biggest room in the world is room for improvement." Please, no matter how great you are, learn your tunes like everyone else.

Other musicians are intimidated by singers or may feel inferior to other musicians. If you're the band leader, remember that it's your job to hire great musicians, hopefully much better than you are, so don't be intimidated.

After years of trying to get my shit together, and of leading countless bands, I realized many important things. If you have a plan and you're super organized, most people will follow your instructions because they don't have a plan of their own, and they trust in you and what you are laying out. This enables you to easily take charge, to guide your musicians, to handle rehearsals, and to speak with confidence, even if you're not the most talented person in the room. This kind of preparation eliminates resistance, negativity, and an attitude masked by silences from shit disturbers who are quick to judge that they could do better than you.

Harmony

There's a common saying in the music industry: the real singers are the backup singers. They can hear the third and the fifth above the lead and harmonize perfectly.

Because harmonies are so difficult to learn and remember, I suggest video recording the rehearsals with your phone, so singers can practice their parts on their own at home. You can also use lyrics sheets to help singers harmonize. For example, you can highlight, underline, or bold the words on the lyrics sheet that are supposed to be harmonized. This way they don't have to sing the entire verse to get to the three words that are being harmonized.

They can just ask if they are singing the first, third, or fifth word and then get to it.

Whether you're using a form or lyrics sheet, remember this: it's okay to bring them to rehearsal just in case, but by the time you walk onstage, everyone should know everything about the song, from beginning to end. Fix it in the factory, not in the performance.

Build Your Set

When you're playing a gig, you have to remember that you're playing for a varied audience. Some people in the crowd like rock, some like funk, others like reggae. Even if you are playing at a blues-only bar, the blues has different eras. I would play the right genre at a rock club, but when I played the latest rock tune of the day, the middle-aged people would stand there bored to tears because they didn't recognize the song.

If you don't throw in a little something for everyone, you'll isolate an entire part of your audience. This means mixing up genres as well as eras within those styles. Again, work this out ahead of time. Don't mix your set so that you play seven reggae songs in a row, or all your rock fans leave before you get to their music. If you have funk songs throughout the set, but they're all from the seventies, you're going to lose the younger funk crowd. Plan it so that by the time you play the third song in your set, the majority of your audience is happy and reassured that you'll most likely get to their favorite styles.

Along with genre, style, and era, you also want to picture the shape of the letter W when you create your set lists. For your first song, pick something that gets the show started at a peak with the audience hyped, or at least fully engaged if you're not going for a "hyped" atmosphere. Not every song makes the audience react the same way, so you naturally see a dip. The trick is to get the dip in the right place—not in the middle, where the audience will get bored and might leave early, thinking your set is all downhill from there, and not at the end, where the audience will remember you for your worst song. The low points should be between the beginning and the middle, then between the middle and the end, just like a W (see Figure 6.4).

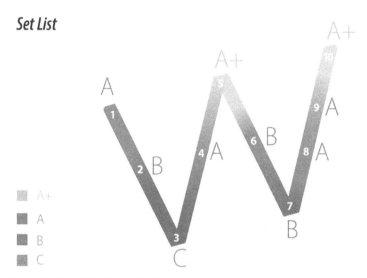

Figure 6.4. Sample Set List in the Shape of a W

With this shape in mind, look at your tunes and rate them: A+, A, B, C. Your A+ and A songs should form the peaks and your Cs the low points, with Bs filling in the gaps in between.

Some songs are A or A+ simply because they are so popular that even if a monkey played them, everyone would jump on the dance floor. Other times, I have to see the artist's delivery of a song and look for a consistent reaction from the audience before I'm confident to say it's an A+. Usually, it's a mixture of delivery and overall popularity of a tune that makes the decision.

B tunes give your audience a bit of a breather. They release the tension. You can't have seven or eight A songs in a row or you'll drain your audience. B tunes are enjoyable, but no one is shouting. This lower-energy vibe also encourages people to take a break and get more drinks, which is crucial for the owner and staff. You need to find a balance between keeping your audience engaged, entertained, dancing, and drinking.

I typically try to get rid of the Cs. Once I have enough songs that are Bs and As, I cut the worst ones and elevate the entire set.

Tempo is also important for the flow of the set, and tempo changes must be done strategically. If you start the set at 80 beats per minute (BPM), don't jump to 120 and then immediately down to 65 or 70 BPM. Build a set that creates a flow and an atmosphere that doesn't jerk around the audience's emotions. You might build to a high-energy tune and then play a ballad and stay slower for a couple songs before building back up.

My bandmates and I had all our tunes in a spreadsheet. We organized it by letter grade, era, and genre. Using our powers of organization, we could then say, "This A+ song works for the ending, these Bs and Cs work on the dips, and these As work at the beginning and the middle." If you follow this simple trick, you've got your whole show right there. The drama of, "Is the audience going to like this one?" is taken right out of the equation. You already know what works, and you can build other sets with a much higher rate of success. When you find a song that's an A+, find a "twin tune" that has a similar feeling, tempo, and delivery. It will most likely give you the same effect. When I'm writing four shows for the next four weeks, I know that there are three or four twin tunes for each song. I use those to create the same feeling and atmosphere over and over, week after week.

Keep in mind that most bars will ask for "forty-five/fifteen" in your sets—forty-five minutes onstage and fifteen minutes off. Most musicians lose concentration after about forty minutes, which averages out to about ten songs. The same goes for the audience. If you play too long, they'll get worn out.

I've found the sweet spot to be a twenty-minute break and usually negotiate for forty/twenty—forty minutes of playing and a twenty-minute break. That still works out to about ten songs per set.

I don't care about finishing our last set at 1:30 a.m. instead of 1:00 a.m., but I'm *very* against playing sixty- or seventy-minute sets; I'd rather play for forty minutes, take a break, and then play another thirty-minute set. Typically, I will tell the owner that they get a total of three hours of playing time and we discuss how to break up the sets. This is part of what you should get in writing before you ever step onstage.

Emceeing

Most musicians don't know how to talk to the audience. Because they're performers, you'd think that welcoming people at the start of the show and thanking them at the end would come easy, but it doesn't. For whatever reason, many musicians get intimidated and flustered at the thought of speaking to the crowd.

That's why you must practice emceeing ahead of time. I'm begging you to go ahead and suck all you can at these greetings at rehearsal, so that you can feel more and more at ease before you actually go onstage. It will feel awkward at first, but the more you practice, the more natural it will feel.

To practice emceeing, I wrote names of our regulars and stuck them on their favorite chairs during rehearsals. By that point we had started playing regularly at certain clubs, so we knew many of our loyal fans by name. Even if you're not there yet, you can practice talking to empty chairs with random names. Look at each chair with a smile and a friendly expression and welcome them. You will probably find this extremely difficult at the beginning because you're talking to nobody, but after a few times it will become a natural part of your rehearsals.

If you don't know what to say, write it out. Think of it as a song, presented with high energy, rather than a speech given at a board meeting. What's the verse? What's the tune? What's the rhythm of the words? "Hey, baby, I saw you yesterday. Glad to have you back." Or "Good evening, ladies and gentlemen, welcome. I hope you're having a really good time tonight." Boom. The drummer taps his sticks, the bass drops the groove, and you're off.

When you're emceeing, you're almost demanding a particular reaction from the audience. As if you're *telling* them to have a good time, not asking. At the end of a set, don't say, "We'll be back in twenty minutes" or some other exact time; just say, "Thank you very much. We'll be back very shortly. Don't you go anywhere."

James Brown understood the importance of this concept. He paid Danny Ray a full-time salary just to be the emcee for his band. His only job was to get the audience raving before the band came out. And it was all in his presentation: "Ladies and gentlemen! It's my pleasure to present to *you*, the *hardest* working man in show business! The *Godfather* of Soul! Put your hands together for James Brown! James Brown! James Brown!" And the crowd went wild.

The success of the show depends on the mood, the atmosphere, right from the beginning. If you come onstage with no energy and whisper into the microphone, "Hey, everybody. Thanks for coming out," you've set the tone for the entire evening. Learn to emcee. It's extremely important and can make or break the success of a performance.

Pre-Recorded Tracks

Back in the day, if you were listening to the Beatles, most of the time, you'd hear two guitars, bass, and drums—and those were the only instruments that you needed to re-create that sound. Today, far more instruments are used to give you the music you enjoy, but bands like yours that are re-creating those sounds have at most vocals, drums, guitar, bass, and keyboard. So the question is, how will you play the horn or violin parts from the recording onstage? You can easily use pre-recorded tracks and play along to them at the gig.

Some musicians take issue with the audience hearing an instrument that's not being played live onstage. That's okay. I used to be one of those musicians. But since then I've found that I could never do justice to the original tunes with only the available instruments onstage. Plus, in today's music, bands are creating custom sounds that aren't found in the presets of a keyboard. Take the classic tune "Smooth" by Santana. The recording of that basic rock song has *over one hundred* tracks layered on top of each other to make it sound live and full. A tune like that is *impossible* to reproduce. Basically, tracks are a tool and have become the norm and can save your ass when trying to play a popular tune.

In addition, most venues are not using the best sound system in the world. Your bass and drums can't reproduce the full-bodied sounds that the track can bring to your audience's expectations of the original songs as they know them. Before we started using tracks, a DJ beat our sound every time because he had the full song with all the instruments at his disposal. This gave him a huge advantage sound-wise because he belted out such a rich, full sound that filled the dance floor with people. When the time came for us to go back onstage for our next set, having a third of the volume and power that the DJ just provided, we'd pale in comparison, and the dance floor would empty almost immediately. No fault of our own; we just couldn't compete.

Using tracks leveled the playing field as we transitioned throughout the evening between us and the DJ. Being at the same sound level made such transitions seamless, kept the dance floor flowing, and made it so much easier for us to keep our audience engaged and happy. But perhaps the greatest advantage of using tracks comes from its consistent tempo. Before tracks were used in live performances, everyone depended on the drummer to remember the exact tempo for every tune *and* to keep that tempo throughout the entire song. Naturally, the drummer would at times count off a song a bit faster or slower, as it is very difficult to remember the speed of a tune in your head. Because of a long list of variables, he might also rush or slow down in the middle of the tune, and the band just had to play along.

Tracks solved this issue once and for all. The tempo was now predetermined in a recording, and the entire band, drummer included, would play with it onstage. In my band, this stopped three years of fighting that resulted from changing tempo: when the song slowed down, the singer would get nervous, then yell at the drummer for slowing down or rushing, then the drummer would get defensive. It was a mess.

Tracks don't care about anyone's emotions. Tracks bring consistency. They play the same exact tempo for the entire three and a half minutes, and nobody can blame anyone anymore. All pressures are off the drummer, and everybody's happy. Problem solved.

Playing tracks during your show also has a few added benefits regarding the intro and outro of each song. As with everything else mentioned in this section, you have to practice using tracks during rehearsals, long before you ever try it onstage.

Intro

Musicians get nervous when they don't know what song is coming up, and it's noticeable onstage. They start looking at each other, stand awkwardly, go check the set list. All of these actions make the band look unprepared and unprofessional.

I wanted my musicians to look at the crowd, not at each other, so I started using tracks to introduce each song. Every tune has a unique musical ID—a unique sound that belongs only to that song. Once band members heard that measure on the track, they knew right away what song was coming up. Then the drummer knew to come in on the second measure to lead in the band. The tune started, the band kicked in, and off we went, with everyone knowing what song they're playing and who's singing it, without taking one look at each other.

Musicians used to argue with me about using tracks. It is true that the track may sometimes limit a musician's freedom and creativity, but you can easily find ways around that, and the benefits far outweigh the limits. The song intros are not the time to get creative. They have a very specific role: one measure to ID the song and let the band know what song is coming up, and another measure to set up the feel and the tune and bring the band confidently on the one. If you want a consistent show and repeat gigs, use tracks.

Outro

In our early days, the band would argue for a half hour over the ending of a song. The song itself was easy. Everybody agreed where the verses and choruses were, but the endings were much more subjective.

The ending of the song only serves one purpose: to get applause. So rather than waste time arguing about an ending—remember, your band is not a democracy!—I started assigning *one* person the task of figuring out the ending. Then it was just like using form. Everybody knew that Mike was in charge of the ending, and it would be already decided ahead of time. Sometimes people wouldn't like a particular ending, but at least someone was in charge. If someone complained, I'd make them do three endings themselves. It humbled them really fast.

Endings are decisive and should scream the song just ended. They should be as clear as daylight because you don't want people to hesitate and wonder, *Do we clap now?* You also don't want to end in a staccato at the end of four. A sudden staccato stop on the end four can be cool on an album, but it catches an audience by surprise, which you don't want. Oftentimes, people judge how good a band is by how loud the applause is, so make the ending obvious so that everyone explodes at the same time once the song is over.

Don't worry if some of your endings seem repetitive. Think about every blues song ever written. Even people who aren't musicians can recognize the end of a blues song by the very last note. As I said of the intro, the song ending is no place for creativity, so just like the intro, write out all the endings, put them in the track, and you'll have them forever. Remember, a definite ending serves only one purpose: it lets people know that the song is over, that it's time to clap and cheer. Nothing else. Put your creativity in your showstoppers, and have a scripted way to end your songs.

Transitions

The transition between songs is like passing the baton in a relay race: the person singing should seamlessly hand over the audience's attention to the next performer, usually another singer, making sure the next person is in tune and ready to grab it. If you're singing two songs in a row, make sure that you keep your audience captivated by your performance until it's someone else's turn to take over. It's a team effort to keep the audience's attention.

Here's one way to engage your audience and keep them on the dance floor during a transition: Say the lead singer finishes at a peak in the set W. Have her move forward slightly, leaning toward the crowd, and then have the rest of the musicians move forward with her in the last eight measures of the song until everyone is standing at the edge of the stage, leaning over and engaging the crowd. Everyone in the band picks a few customers and makes eye contact. They stay there until the next song starts, and when it does, the audience will still be dancing, four to six measures into the new song. Once the dance floor is secured, it's safe for everyone in the band to move back into position.

Remember the 80/20 principle: 80 percent of the people on the dance floor will wait until a song is over and then leave between songs. What you want to do is keep the crowd excited and fixated on the band. Some people will leave—there's nothing you can do about that—but some will rush to the stage to dance to the new song. The best scenario is to have more people come in than leave and keep your dance floor packed. An empty dance floor is a lonely place.

Even if you are not playing to a dance floor, you still need to show a "changing of the guard." As the singers swap places, have some musicians move forward or take a few steps sideways while others move back. This type of movement creates a visual flow, which stimulates the audience's attention and eliminates the possibility of boredom. In their eyes and minds, it shows that the band has rehearsed transitions from song to song and that cares about their performance. Through well-rehearsed transitions, you catch the audience's eye, so that they know when to clap and are more likely to remain on the dance floor.

Volume

Nobody pays attention to volume in rehearsal because the volume sounds perfect when there's no adrenaline, no alcohol, no jumping up and down, and no audience chatter. So when the band gets onstage, they have no idea what the volume should be.

In general, if you keep the stage volume low and comfortable, your musicians can play with finesse instead of bashing their instruments trying to be loud enough for the audience. The singers can hear themselves and have more control over their voices. Controlled stage volume makes for a much more pleasant evening. A good test to find the right volume during rehearsal is to have the band play and see if the singer and drummer can talk to each other. If they can, you're good to go.

It's natural for the band to start getting louder over the course of a song and an evening because the more people drink, the louder they talk and the higher their adrenaline flows. People get excited. No matter what, the volume still needs to be controlled, otherwise the drummer will start to play louder, the bass will turn up his amp, and then the singers will start yelling, sometimes to the point of fearing they are abusing their voices. If that happens, they'll lose finesse and pitch, they'll get pissed off, and this doesn't make for a good-sounding band.

A great way to control the volume mid-song is to already have signals prepared that everyone knows.

Signals

Signals can be used to communicate between certain musicians or within the band as a whole while still keeping the groove, the energy, and the song going. As a drummer, I used to subtly play a predetermined cowbell figure to tell the band when I felt that we were getting louder. When they heard it, all of the musicians knew they needed to drop their volume by 20 percent on the next measure and to coast at that volume. If you're a guitarist, you can signal by tapping your shoulder. If you're the musical director, you can touch your head. Any signal works as long as you discuss it beforehand and rehearse it so that it's clear to the entire band—and so that no one gets offended when the signal to lower the volume is given. It's just a friendly reminder for the sake of creating the most enjoyable experience for everyone. The real genius of nonverbal signals is that the audience is completely unaware. There is no distraction. They just get to enjoy the show.

On many nights, one of the band members would be on fire and would feel like the track was holding them back. Signals allowed us to improvise. If I was up front singing and the guitar player next to me was hot, without even looking back, I would make a signal and Marc, who was on drums, would immediately stop the track, so the guitarist could do his thing. This freedom enabled us to really jam and do whatever we wanted. We'd feature our singers or give some of our musicians longer solos or invite audience participation. It was so satisfying and exhilarating. Word of caution, though: if you leave the structure of the tune, you'd better know what you're doing to get back on track once you're done with the free form.

If you're using pre-recorded tracks, it's possible that something could go wrong. We had a signal for this situation too. I would make a gesture without looking back, and Marc would know how to end the tune and dial up the next. If we were losing the audience, I had a signal that meant everyone should move up onstage. We even had a signal if one of us recognized that we were losing the audience but the others didn't: Marc would play something we had agreed upon that meant "engage the audience's attention immediately." For example, instead of playing the snare on two and four, which happens in 99 percent of all modern tunes, he would play the snare on all quarter notes, loud and crisp. It sent the signal, and everyone moved forward to save the floor.

Nonverbal signals like this come in handy in many other situations: rowdy crowds, nervous bandmates, and more. It would be wonderful if all of your shows went as planned, just like you practiced them during rehearsals, but shit happens. Rather than panic, practice subtle signals that communicate the message without skipping a beat—and without showing your frustration on your faces. Angry looks or gestures onstage look very unprofessional. Even a giggle with your buddy onstage because of a mistake someone made can be misunderstood by the audience. They might think you're laughing at them.

After you come up with your signals, document them, teach them to every band member, and rehearse them to death. That way you'll be prepared no matter what happens.

HOW TO RUN A REHEARSAL

Rehearsal is everything. It's where you assemble the show—all the songs, all the individual parts, all the dance moves, everything. If you are the one running the rehearsal, you'd better be on time, and you'd better know what you're going to cover inside out. The following will give you an outline to follow to make the most of your rehearsals.

Pre-Rehearsal Brief

I like to start with coffee about ten minutes before the brief starts. This is downtime, the calm before the storm, so I fool around and crack jokes, but when the brief starts, I am dead serious. There's no more messing around. We've got a job to do and a great show to put together.

The pre-rehearsal brief should happen every single rehearsal, even if you rehearse every day and you have been playing together for years. The brief should take place a good twenty to thirty minutes before anyone plays a single note. Based on experience, ten minutes before won't cut it because everyone will all of a sudden have last-minute emergencies before you drop the first beat.

Here's an example of what you can say:

Hi, everyone. The rehearsal will start in a few minutes. I value your time, and our time is limited, so let's make it extremely productive. If you'd be so kind, let's follow these guidelines in order to get to it and get the most out of this rehearsal.

Please remember that the lyrics and forms are there for reference and to make it easier to communicate with each other, but there is no reading when we rehearse. If you don't know the tunes by now, then 100 percent you will not be ready for the show by this evening. We want our show to be top-notch, and whatever happens here is what will happen onstage tonight, so let's do this and make it fantastic. The rehearsal is the show.

- *Downbeat is 3:00 p.m. (all instruments tuned; sound system turned on; monitors, amps, and microphones checked; all four tools at arm's length).*
- *Please put your phones on "do not disturb" and set them aside until you need them to record something or take a note.*
- *Please don't noodle on your instruments while we're talking.*
- *Please go to the washroom now. Get your water and whatever you need.*

- *Have your four tools ready now: forms, tracks, originals, lyrics.*
- *Please don't talk and ask questions out of turn. I promise I will get to each one of you and we'll attend to all your concerns.*
- *If we are discussing harmonies, the rhythm section should pay attention, and if we are practicing the groove, singers should pay attention. After all, it's the sum of all parts that make the tune, and we should all be very familiar with each other's parts.*

After your brief and after everyone has used the washroom, it's time to get to work.

The Rehearsal

Use the form to talk through each tune, whether the form is scribbled or done in a music software. Singers can follow with the lyrics. Have everyone jot down anything that needs to be added or corrected so that the form and lyrics now match.

For instance, singers usually just have words on their lyrics page, but before coming to rehearsal, they should have inserted notes like "Guitar solo—sixteen bars after chorus two." On the other hand, musicians should have scribbled the first few words of verse two on the form, something like "We look for love." That way, everyone can communicate clearly during rehearsal because everyone is on the same page.

The form of a basic tune would look something like this:

- ID—1 bar
- Drum lead-in—1 bar
- Intro—8 bars
- Verse 1—8 bars
- Chorus 1—8 bars
- Verse 2—8 bars
- Chorus 2—8 bars
- Bridge interlude—8 bars
- Guitar solo—16 bars
- Chorus 3—8 bars
- Chorus 4—8 bars
- Outro—2 bars

After talking through each tune, it's time to break up and work on different parts.

Rhythm Section

Start by having the musicians run through the tune: the intro, the ending, any hits in the middle, any unique parts. They practice until they get each part right. Don't run the verses and choruses yet; you'll do that next.

Once all the unique and ad hoc parts have been worked out as a band, isolate each instrument and have them play one verse and one chorus alone to bring all the attention to that instrument and make sure it sits and it's grooving. Having a musician play his part alone while everyone else is listening has a couple of benefits: (1) All of the other musicians are now very intimate with that instrument's parts because they are not busy playing themselves; they are just listening and truly hearing. (2) Band members quickly learn that they will have to play alone while everyone else is watching.

I found that isolations alone made everyone much more conscious and brought the level of concentration up tenfold. It also caused everyone to pay special attention to learning their parts very well ahead of rehearsals.

Singers

Now that the band parts are solid and grooving, bring the singers into the fold and walk through the same process. Isolate the lead singer, that is, give him his key and have him sing the whole verse and a chorus alone, with no instruments. The singers will feel self-conscious and awkward at first, but that's okay. They'll get used to it, and their confidence will go through the roof.

Now the whole band is watching the singer go through his parts, which is another helpful exercise. Many musicians don't pay attention to the singer's phrasing or the lyrics, and isolations help them do that. This awareness can help them avoid overplaying and burying the melody.

After you go through the lead singers, have the backup singers do the same.

Put It All Together

Once you finish working with each individual, count it off and bring everyone in. It should fit like a glove because all the parts were perfected individually first.

If there are some mistakes, identify the instrument and part of the tune, and then go over only the measures with the mistakes and only the instruments that made the mistakes. Don't run the whole tune down again with everyone playing.

Once the parts are cleaned up, then run the whole tune down again with the whole band. Once you like what you hear, have someone take their phone out and video record the band running down the polished tune, and share it with everyone, so they can review anytime as need be.

Document Everything

By the end of this book, you're going to have a new mantra: document everything. All of your decisions about musical mechanics—forms, lyrics sheets, set lists, signals, transitions, briefing the band, rehearsal—must be documented. That is how you create and implement a fail-proof system.

After it's documented once, it's copy, paste, and repeat over and over again.

Many musicians prefer using pen and paper for taking notes and jotting down reminders. That's fine as they get started, but handwritten notes can be messy and disconnected, and paper can be misplaced. I recommend moving to digital filing for its benefits in organization, sharing, and search abilities.

Obviously, when you name your file, name it in a way that is intuitive, something that will be easy for you to remember and find six months or a year from now. It also has to make sense to someone else, who has no idea how you named the file. For example, don't write "Uptown" or "UTF"; write out the whole name "Uptown Funk," so there is no confusion. But even that's not enough. Will you remember whether this is the form or track? How will someone else know? Better to write something like "Uptown Funk - Form" or "Uptown Funk - Lyrics." If you forget to file items in their designated folders, then naming properly becomes your savior. I use a folder numbering system. Numbering the folders, instead of alphabetizing them, keeps everything neat and orderly, as you can see in Figure 6.5.

Now we're moving on to the visual presentation aspect of your gig, which you'll also want to document using your new system.

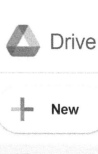

Drive

+ **New**

▾ ▣ **My Drive**

> ▸ 📁 **Business**
> ▸ 📁 **Personal**

2 Main folders

▸ 🖥 Computers

👥 Shared with me

🕐 Recent

☆ Starred

🗑 Trash

☁ Storage

10 MB of 15 GB used

(1/3)

Figure 6.5a. Sample Folder Numbering System

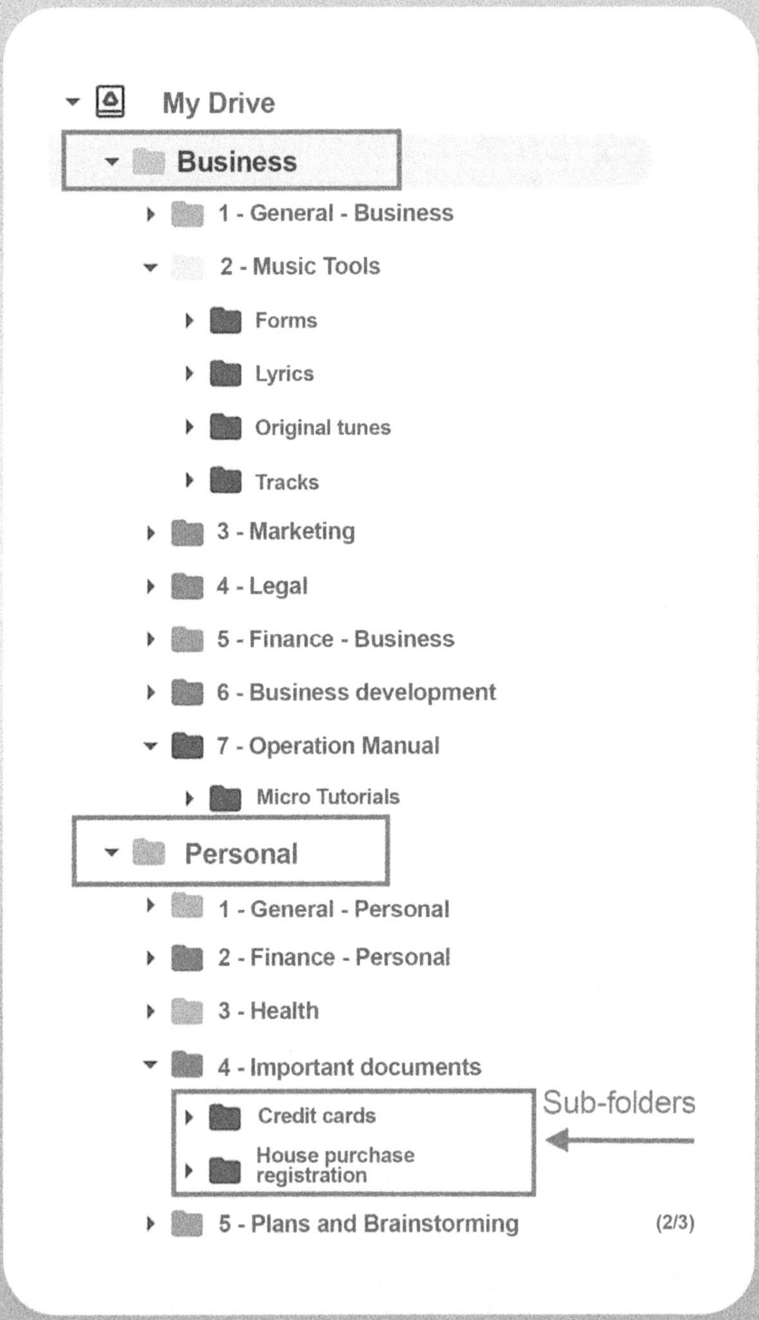
My Drive
Business
1 - General - Business
2 - Music Tools
Forms
Lyrics
Original tunes
Tracks
3 - Marketing
4 - Legal
5 - Finance - Business
6 - Business development
7 - Operation Manual
Micro Tutorials
Personal
1 - General - Personal
2 - Finance - Personal
3 - Health
4 - Important documents
Credit cards
House purchase registration
Sub-folders
5 - Plans and Brainstorming
(2/3)

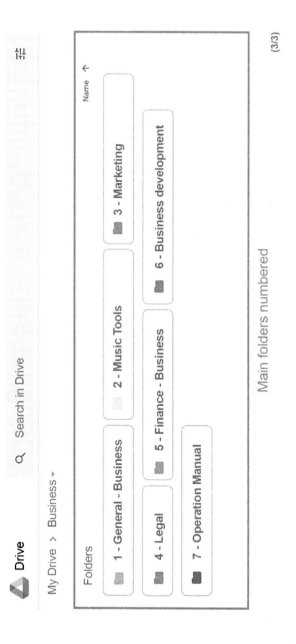

Main folders numbered

PRESENTATION

Sometimes people feel like presentation means they have to act like a K-pop band, jumping up and down, and dancing to intricate choreographies. That's not always the case. Presentation starts the moment you set foot onstage and includes your demeanor, confidence, attitude, stance as you play your instrument, facial expressions, and even your smile.

Keith Richards doesn't dance like Mick Jagger, but he still has a very strong vibe, a way of moving his body that is natural to him, and it's coming from his heart, and the audience can't take their eyes off him.

You may not be the best dancer, but like Keith Richards, you have the opportunity to create your own vibe, your own style, so take the time to figure out what that is.

At a live show, people don't just listen to the music with their ears; they listen with their eyes too. And they're not just watching—they're staring intensely, analyzing and judging your every move. If you stand in the same place the whole time with the same passive look on your face, the audience is probably going to think, *Man, this guy is not into it.* Or, *What a dud.*

Like every other part of your performance, presentation requires practice.

Move Air

Sometimes I tell my bandmates, "You've gotta move air." In other words, the swiftness of your movements should create a breeze. Don't walk without purpose. Be energized. Move your ass. Move some air.

When Beyoncé performs, she's all over the place. Jennifer Lopez and Mick Jagger—they both move air, man. And some of them create hurricanes onstage, as part of their captivating and memorable performances.

Basically, you're not going to excite any of your fans if you sway like Frank Sinatra to an explosive Bruno Mars tune. Your level of energy and high intensity should always match the style of the song. That's the only way you'll have the power to entice the crowd to join the party as they make their way to the dance floor.

The Story of the Song

If you're a non-vocalist, you might be thinking, *Why are we spending so much time talking about the singers' parts?* That's because most of your audience connects with the lyrics. Just pay attention when you're performing, and you'll see that they sing along because they all know the words.

That's why it's important for *all* band members to understand the story of the song. If you don't know what the lyrics are really all about, then you could be giving the wrong impression onstage. Your body language might not match the meaning behind the words. Or your tone might match the tune but not the message. It's like telling someone "I love you" while rolling your eyes. It doesn't add up.

Let's say a girl wrote a song about a cheating boyfriend. During rehearsal, if our lead singer performed this song while smiling, trying to connect with our pretend audience, I would stop the performance and ask, "What are you doing? This girl is pissed off. This guy cheated on her. How can you be nice when you're singing about him? Talk to him as if you want to punch him in the head."

The same applies to the entire band. The audience is watching everyone's facial expressions and body language, so you all have to make sure that you're supporting the story and its nuances throughout the song.

Video

These days, it's easy to record a rehearsal. When I first started, I had to have someone else hold an actual old-school video camera to tape our performance. Now you can just whip out your smartphone, lean it on something, and press record.

Videos of your rehearsal are not simply a nice souvenir to have. This is mandatory. What you think you look like when you're performing and what the audience sees are often two different things, and that will become clear when you see yourself on camera.

Video recording your shows and reviewing them is the fastest way to improve your band. It's like practice on steroids. It's the only way to see yourself like the audience sees you. Once you sit down and watch yourself on camera, you can spot even the tiniest of mistakes and fix them immediately.

Warning: you probably won't like what you see when you watch yourself. But if you can record your performance and get past the first two weeks of cringing every time you watch, then you'll start to see yourself the way the audience does. They're not seeing you with your preconceived notions and all the judgment you reserve for yourself. To them, you're just some guy or girl who is up onstage. The question is, are you delivering the experience you intended for them to see? Are you causing people to feel the emotions you want them to feel, whether that's happiness, anger, or sentimentality? Or do you have habits and quirks that are taking away from that experience?

When reviewing your performances, put your emotions aside and pretend you're critiquing another artist. In his documentary *This Is It*, Michael Jackson watches a recording of his performance and refers to himself in third person. When he sees something he doesn't like he says, "I don't like how he did that," as if he is talking about someone else. It's not you in the video; it's the artist, and you're trying to fix the way he appears onstage.

When you watch the video, take note of little ticks that might be distracting to the audience, and then take steps to fix them. For example, take a look at your arms. Do you drop them straight down by your sides? Merely lifting them to waist height looks less stiff.

Here are some big no-nos that you should look for and eliminate:

- Gum chewing
- Giggling
- Staring passively at someone in the crowd
- Lip-synching a song while someone else is singing
- Looking annoyed because you can't hear yourself
- Sniggering
- Blocking your ears and wincing when the band gets too loud at times
- Looking frustrated or unhappy, maybe because your bandmate messed up

Video will capture all of this and more. Rehearsals are the perfect place to start changing your presentations in all these little ways, and mainly because videos don't lie.

FINISH THE JOB

When my son, Julian, was five years old, I used to give him little chores, so he could feel purposeful and proud that he was helping me. One day that chore was to sharpen a pencil. When he was done, I picked up the pencil and asked, "Does this pencil look sharpened to you?"

"No," he said sheepishly.

"Okay. Can you please sharpen the pencil properly?"

Julian took the pencil, put it in the sharpener, and turned it twice. Click. Click. That was all it took. Just two more clicks for a perfectly sharpened pencil.

The difference between a good gig and a great one is often just as small, but many bands fail to put in the "two more clicks" to get there. Instead they settle for a good-enough show—the same half-assed performance they give at rehearsals.

If you want to stand out, if you want to gig for life, you have to put in those two clicks and finish the job. Spend the extra time working on intros and outros. Practice moving air. Work on controlling your volume, and use your signals and cues. Put in the extra 20 percent that many bands don't; that's where the magic lives. That's how you will outshine the competition, and that's why you'll get hired over and over again.

You've worked on you, you've put a band together, you've booked a gig—don't stop now! Rehearse, rehearse, rehearse. It all leads to the stage, the most sacred place, the whole reason why you do what you do. The stage is where you connect with the fourth part of your ecosystem—your fans.

WORK IT OUT

Sit down and think through your rehearsals. You have three hours. How many tunes will you work through? How will you rehearse the harmonies? The rhythm section? The intros and outros? Are you playing that song as is or adding a solo or a rap section, or mixing two tunes? How will you walk on and offstage?

Work out every single step of the rehearsal, from hello to goodnight. If you write these pointers down once, you'll use that structure for the rest of your life. You can always tweak here and there. Set up the process now, document it, systematize it. Rehearsals are the show. Take them very seriously.

Write a post sharing what you have learned and how you improved the rehearsal process, and tag me with #prepareforyourgig #gigforlife.

FANS

STAGE TIME

Back in the early eighties, I was living in Ottawa, taking music lessons, and working at the pizzeria that I had bought when I was seventeen. One of my friends turned me on to Motown and the music of Junior Walker, so when I heard he was coming to our little town, I went to see him play.

The place was packed. The energy was high. And Junior Walker was absolutely killing it onstage. It was one of those moments that you live for as a musician and remember for the rest of your life, when the audience and the band become one. A wall of emotion hit me like a tsunami. I was drowning, and I loved it.

Junior Walker was playing a second show that same night at the same venue a few hours later, and I really wanted to go back and share the experience with someone, anyone. I went home and begged every family member and friend I could find. Finally, a close family friend accepted the invitation. As we drove to the club, I talked his ear off the whole time. "Oh man, this show's going to be amazing. You're going to love it!"

The show started, and I kept waiting for that same energy and connection. This time, however, there was no tsunami, not even a wave of emotion to surf on. The show sucked. I don't know what happened between show one and show two, but it seemed like a completely different band. The whole night my friend gave me the side eye, forcing a clap between songs out of politeness. I was so embarrassed.

Junior Walker had promised a certain kind of performance, but he and the band did not deliver during the second show. I made a promise to myself right then and there: *From the day I become a professional musician, I will always give 100 percent. I will never let down my fans.*

I'm not the world's best musician, not by a long shot. But every time I walked onstage, I left everything out there. I dropped every ounce of talent God gave me, and I don't think anyone that has seen my band play would disagree. I delivered on my promise every single time.

The stage is a sacred place. It is the platform where you perform a ritual, where you cast a spell that makes your relationship with the audience come to life. The stage is the whole reason why you've done everything in your power to become a musician. It's the reason for every dollar spent on equipment, private lessons, and university studies. It's the reason for every minute spent practicing on your own or in rehearsal. This is it.

When you disrespect the stage—by looking at your watch, by packing up before the lights even go off, by not taking a few moments to go shake some hands and to thank people for coming and acknowledging your job well done, by not giving 100 percent every single time—it ruins the experience for everyone. Everything you worked so hard to cultivate over the past weeks, months, and years goes up in smoke.

This track will help you avoid that fiasco.

WHY ARE YOU HERE?

Before you read any further, ask yourself this question: Why are you here? Why are you putting in these long hours to get onstage?

If you say, "I need the money," you are in the wrong domain. I can think of thousands of jobs that would pay you so much better. If you say, "I love music," "I hate my day job," "I love traveling"—basically, if your answer is about you—then you're on the wrong track.

When it comes to the stage, there's only one right answer to that question: the audience. Why else would you walk onstage? If the audience is irrelevant, then you can play anywhere—in your garage, in your mom's backyard, at your brother's wedding reception. But any time you walk onstage, there is an audience. That's why you're there.

When you're onstage, you have the power to unite strangers' emotions in one single experience: dancing, singing, waving their arms. People walk in with so many different moods based on so many different experiences from whatever day they've had. Through your talents and skills, you and your band have the power to change everyone's mood and to create a euphoric atmosphere that can be shared by all. I've never experienced anything more powerful than when the crowd and the musicians become one, as I experienced at the first Junior Walker concert.

If you understand that your ultimate goal is to touch the audience and to bring them into one shared experience, then you will treat the stage as your sacred ground. The tips that follow are discussed with that focus in mind, from the moment you walk onstage until the moment you walk off.

THE STAGE, BEGINNING TO END

In the next track, Floor Time, we'll talk about your relationships with fans between and after sets. For now, we're going to focus on your relationship while you are on that sacred stage.

Let's walk through that experience, from before you ever set foot on the stage until you're briefing about your performance the next day. Every aspect is important to keeping the stage sacred.

You Chose This Business, So Embrace It

First, a little tough love: If you can't stand the sight of blood, don't become a surgeon. If you don't want to slap yourself into a good mood at the first minute of showtime every night, don't become a musician. No one cares about your problems. When you hit the stage, you need to be ready to rock no matter what's going on in your personal life. Your job is to make other people happy, to help them forget their problems. This is the life you chose, so get on with it, or quit. You can't have both. Once you hit the stage it's never about you. It's about your audience. It's about delivering the experience you promise, whether that's an evening of smooth jazz or a night of slamming dance music.

Create a Pre-Show Ritual

Michael Jordan once said that he won basketball games before they had even started. Prior to stepping on the court, he would play through the entire game in his head. You don't have to be the greatest basketball player to think like that. I took the same approach with my gigs. About an hour and a half before the show, I would isolate myself and think about everything I was about to do.

During that time, I thought through exactly what I was going to say to the band and how I would walk onstage.

I envisioned myself playing all the songs in the first set, then in the second. I thought about how I would speak to the audience on the floor. I thought through every aspect of the show, start to finish. I even thought through my trigger songs and which song I would use for an encore.

You may not know who exactly will be at the gig, but you do know that at least one rowdy person, shy person, and drunk person will be there. You can see the energy of the room in your mind's eye. You know your band and which members may become passive throughout the course of the evening. You know yourself and which notes you often miss and what songs don't groove as well. Walk through these aspects in your mind enough times, and you'll be amazed at how night after night the show goes *exactly* the way you envisioned it, just like the movie you wrote in your head.

Even if I had to go to the washroom and be by myself for four minutes, I would do it. I needed that time alone to put myself in the right frame of mind and to walk through how I wanted the evening to go. Taking this time to play it all out in your mind will set the stage, literally, for a better show.

Don't Eat Before the Show

Let's get really specific: if you're going onstage at ten o'clock, don't eat dinner past six. Otherwise, you're going to be in for a long, uncomfortable, burp-filled night. If you

STAGE TIME · 199

have ever eaten within a couple of hours of being onstage, you know exactly what I mean. You'll have low energy and constant discomfort, which will affect your concentration. In general, you're going to want to get offstage as quickly as possible.

Give Them a Pep Talk

Just before the show, I used to gather everyone together and say, "Okay guys, the house is full. We've got about two hundred people in the audience. Let's make sure it doesn't get out of hand; the speakers are right in the front, so the dance floor's going to get the full brunt of the sound. Watch the volume. If you don't hear the person next to you, you are too loud. Ready? Let's do this."

Another pep talk I'd give went something like this: "This is the first set. We are not going to blast them. Let's ease into it. Let's stay slick, laid back, and keep the volume low so that people can hear each other."

And yet another went like this: "Stay focused. We are going to unleash hell, balls to the walls, everyone on the dance floor by song three, no matter what it takes. Everyone, stay focused on one thing: full dance floor by song three. Keep your eyes on the target. Now, let's go make somebody happy."

Speak from your heart during these pep talks. Keep it positive and focused on giving the audience a Saturday night performance.

Transition from the DJ

The transition from the DJ to the band and back again is extremely important. You want it to be as seamless as possible, without losing the energy in the room or the people on the dance floor. This takes practice.

One thing that can make this transition not so smooth is the friction that sometimes exists between the band and the DJ. Band members think being a DJ is an easy job—just push play and sit back. DJs think band members are prima donnas—they play a few songs they didn't even write and get undeserved praise.

One way to ease this friction is to take time to build camaraderie with the DJ. He is an important extension of your band. He can make or break the mood of the room between sets, so take time at the beginning of the show to get on the same page so you can work together to give the audience a great experience. Another way to ease friction is to show the DJ some love. At the end of the night, acknowledge his hard work—out loud, into the mic, so everyone can hear you.

Walk On with Purpose

As a way to keep himself and his band focused, one member of a veteran band I put together used to tell me, "Wait till we hit wood, brother." When you hit wood—in other words, when you walk on that stage—you mean business.

All the lonely hours spent practicing, all the challenges, self-doubt, and sacrifices. As musicians, we do all of these things with one thing in mind: hitting wood, walking into the spotlight where we do our thing. Whether you're playing in front of thousands of people from a massive platform or from the floor in front of two people, the stage space is sacred, and the ritual of performing is to be taken seriously. This is where you display what you are all about. What you do every time you step in front of people is what will define you as a musician and performer in everyone's eyes, and most importantly, in your own mind. No matter your skill level or fame, you are a professional. Every night you come to play. Never take the stage, the audience, your fellow musicians, the bar that hired you, or your talent and effort for granted.

When I was living in Ottawa, James Brown came to town for a black and white party. After a band made up of local radio DJs played their tunes and the audience politely clapped, there was silence. The stage lights were lowered. We waited.

Then James Brown's musicians walked onstage, one at a time, not one of them smiling. They were dressed in pressed black suits, white shirts, and black ties, looking absolutely immaculate, right down to their army-shined black shoes. They picked up their instruments and stood in place. No one said a word. No one tuned a guitar or tapped the mic for "one, two, testing" nonsense. They all just stood there staring straight ahead—guitarists with hands on the neck of their instruments, two drummers with sticks in their hands and hands on knees, and brass section with their horns held next to their bodies, like soldiers ready to march. They were all focused, serious, and silent.

We were quiet in the audience too, watching and waiting with a sense of "Fasten your seatbelts, something extraordinary is about to happen!" The anticipation in that room was so thick, you could almost touch it. I felt like I was going to faint, and they hadn't even played a single note.

Finally, we heard, "One, two, a one, two, three, four," and the downbeat dropped, and they unleashed a truckload of funk. They played a groove so deep it should have been illegal. If someone in that audience didn't get goosebumps at that moment, they must have already died from the impact. The place absolutely exploded. The walk-on alone set the tone that James Brown, the Godfather of Soul himself, the Hardest Working Man in Show Business, was in the house, and his band was not there to mess around. They were bringing a show that the audience would remember for as long as they live—and James Brown hadn't even walked onstage yet. That was during the early 1980s, and I'm still recovering.

Creating this kind of anticipation and emotion takes serious practice, and it's worth every second of your rehearsals. With this kind of walk-on, you set the tone for the whole evening before you even play a note. If you stroll out nonchalantly and start tuning your instruments while you chat with one another or an audience member, you're taking away from the anticipation that something magical is about to take place.

One way to do it is to let the musicians walk on, play a groove, turn up the heat, and when the time comes, start the tune and let the singer walk out. If it's a slow song played while people are eating and chatting, the singers can walk on elegantly and start singing, but if it's time to rip the place apart, start with a high-energy groove. Let the crowd immediately sense that "shit is going down. Bring on the bubbly, 'cause this is one nasty band. I know I'm skipping work tomorrow!"

One of your musicians could do the Danny Ray thing, introducing your band with the same flair and hype that Ray used to bring out James Brown. Introduce the singers, play some hits, add some drama, bring some excitement. You can achieve this at the concert level, playing for thousands, or with a guitar and singer duo at a cafe. Use your imagination and make the walk-on special. It sets the tone of the evening for the audience, and it also puts the band in the right frame of mind: "We are about to deliver something very special."

After the DJ has handed you the stage, it's time to lay it all out. Now is not the time to tune your instruments and test your mics. When you walk onstage, simply pick up your instruments and stand at the ready, just like James Brown's band—hand on the guitar neck, drumsticks in hand, horns held at the side. There's no need to talk. Your posture communicates that you are ready without saying a word or even glancing around. It shows that you are professionals who are ready to deliver the highest-level performance.

Look at the Audience, Not Your Fingers

Whether you're playing to a crowd of five or fifty, those people came to watch you play, so give them a show they won't forget. Play *to* them, not *at* them. Entertain them. Connect with them. Sometimes that means you should be looking toward their faces, not at your fingers or your instruments.

I know what you're thinking: *Not all music styles demand that. Bruno Mars, sure, but jazz?* It's true; if you play jazz, it's okay if you look at your fingers more often, but you still have to connect with the audience. Jazz icon Herbie Hancock knew this: when I saw him play in Montreal with Jack DeJohnette, he grabbed his Keytar and slid on his knees all the way to center stage. The crowd went crazy. Even Herbie didn't mind a bit of fun.

The key here is that you have to connect with your audience. This might take some practice, so add that to the list of things to rehearse, rehearse, rehearse.

Don't Read Crowd, Lead the Crowd

Some musicians take pride in the fact that they can "read the crowd." They'll say something like, "I know what music to play because I read the crowd, man. I can see what they're feeling."

Well, what happens when one table is feeling mellow because they're conducting business, and another is all hyped up because they're having a bachelorette party? Which part of the room do you read? What group do you play for?

Your job is to know what kind of club you're in and lead the crowd to that party. Period. You're not there to read the room so you can lead them to where they want to go. You're in charge. You're leading the crowd to the experience and emotions that the show is supposed to deliver.

Don't Judge Your Audience

The more you engage your audience, the better you'll see them. When that happens, however, you might be tempted to pass judgment on who and what you see:

- That girl's pretty.
- That guy gives me a bad vibe.
- That guy has on a wedding band, but the girl he's dancing with doesn't.
- That girl was here last week with a different guy.
- Is that a working girl?
- That guy is so drunk. I can't stand him.

It's not your job to judge your audience. Your job is to play.

When you're onstage, you're an apple tree. An apple tree doesn't care who picks its apples. Whether the picker is a working girl, a criminal, a murderer, a cheater, a priest, or an atheist, the apple tree will give out its apples generously, and each one will be crisp and sweet. Your job as a musician is to play music and put on a show, no matter who's in the audience.

Every time you judge someone in the crowd, you are less of a musician. You are less of an entertainer. If you judge someone and stop smiling, then you're no longer giving your best show. You just lowered your standards. Do that enough times, and that lower-standard musician becomes the new you. If you're too focused on the audience, on what each individual member may or may not deserve, then you're not playing your show anymore. Your job is to walk onstage and give that love without judging anyone.

There is no such thing as a boring audience, just boring bands. Remember: the audience didn't come to entertain you and get you out of your rut. They came to relax and feel good, and they hope the band can help make that happen. The minute you catch yourself thinking, *This crowd is so boring*, go look in the mirror, get your shit together, come back, and do your job. Boredom comes from lack of concentration. Stop judging those in front of you, and do your job, your calling. Focus on leaving it all on the stage.

No matter what the atmosphere of the bar is when you start, make it your goal to turn it into something exciting and unforgettable. Take that chaotic pool of emotions, ages, backgrounds, and nationalities, and play in a way that says, "Here, beautiful people, let me show you where we are going tonight. It doesn't matter who you are or what kind of day you've had. I promise you that within minutes, we are all going to be in the same zone, feeling the same way."

Focused musicians hold great power. They can control the mood of any room by casting magical music spells so that everyone has a blast—an evening to remember and to make them want to come back and back again.

Don't Drown Out the Crowd

When you're playing popular songs, it should be easy to get the crowd to sing along. These are popular songs; everyone knows the words to the classics or whatever the latest hit is. It seems like all you'd have to do is yell out, "Everybody!" before the chorus to get the whole room to join in the fun.

When you have multiple speakers and amplifiers, it's easy to drown out the crowd when they try to sing along. To create excitement, the audience has to be able to hear themselves. And for that to happen, you have to get out of the way after you say, "Everybody!" and let the audience belt it out. If you sing along with them through the mic, you'll drown them out and they'll stop singing because they can't hear themselves. So nudge them a little, and then point the mic at them as an invitation to participate.

Another way to get the crowd involved is to do a call and response. When you do this, the same principle applies:

step away from the microphone after you "call" so that the crowd can hear their response, not yours.

Another tip: when you ask a question, always give the answer. If you say, "How's everyone doing tonight?" you're going to get many different answers shouted out—or none at all. Instead, say, "If you're feeling alright, say, 'Yeah,'" and then point the microphone at the crowd while they answer, "Yeah!"

Never Hand Over the Microphone

Although you do want to get the crowd involved, you should never hand over the microphone to anyone in the audience. Doing so just creates chaos. The person may sing too loudly and then hand the mic to their friend, and then you've lost control of the show. That mic is yours and yours only. If you want to let someone belt out a line, fine, but don't let go of the mic.

Give Little Shout-Outs

One sure way to engage your audience is by giving little shout-outs to people in the crowd. If you met someone the last time you played at the bar and they show up to another gig, acknowledge them with a simple, "Roger and Janet are in the house tonight."

If you talked to someone between sets and found out it's their first time, give them a special greeting. If you learned that the group of ladies in the back is celebrating someone's birthday, give her a shout-out: "I see you, birthday girl. Happy birthday! What's up, ladies?"

People like to feel special. The words you use are irrelevant. Do it with your own language and personality. Little acknowledgments like this go a long way to bring the audience into the show and to entice them to come back often.

Don't Jukebox the Crowd

When you get in a groove, you may be tempted to belt out one tune after another. When you do this, however, you can totally overwhelm the audience to the point where they zone out. Don't jukebox—don't play one song after another after another without giving the audience room to breathe. It will feel like you're throwing songs at them instead of playing to them. You might as well be a jukebox. Too much of a good thing can sometimes backfire.

If you realize you're coming at the audience with all of your might and they're starting to zone out, go to the other extreme. Finish your tune and then play a laid-back song or a ballad. Give everyone a chance to breathe for a second. When you have the audience again, you can reboot and get back on track where you left your W.

Dim the Dance Floor

Each venue will have different lighting, some significantly better than others. Make sure that you check it out before the show and figure out how to control the lighting on the dance floor. You want to keep that space dim because people often shy away when the dance floor is too bright. By dimming the lights, you control the mood that you want to create and give people a space to feel safe, to dance their hearts out without feeling self-conscious. If you put too much light on the dance floor, people may want to retreat to a darker area, and that space between your guests and your band can become the gap of death.

Close the Gap of Death

Nothing is worse than when you're playing your heart out at a gig and the dance floor is empty. This happens sometimes, even when you've dimmed the lights, and it can leave a huge knot in your stomach. You know that no matter how good you are, when people come in and see that big empty space on the dance floor, many of them will think, *The band is not that good.* That space can become so large that it starts to kill the mood. The gap of death is real, and it must be closed as quickly as possible (Figure 7.1).

Many musicians don't even notice the gap forming. First, the audience is one foot away from them, then two feet, then five. Then before they know it, the dance floor is empty and they're left thinking, *Holy shit! When did that happen?*

You have to keep your eye on the dance floor at all times. Whenever you see the gap grow wider than a foot, reach out and high five someone or lower the lights even more or get on the mic and say something like, "Get a little closer

Phases of the gap of death

Objective

The Band / Crowd	The Band / Gap of death / Crowd	The Band / Gap of death / Crowd	The Band / Gap of death / Crowd	The Band / Gap of death

Fully crowded — Gap of death starts — Gap of death growing — Gap of death keeps on growing — No crowd

To avoid

Warm, exciting, and inviting atmosphere — to — Very cold and rejective atmostphere

Figure 7.1. The Gap of Death

everyone, we love it when you are up here dancing! It energizes us!" This makes people feel safe and calm. They feel comfortable getting close to you because you managed to close the gap of death.

Sometimes the crowd was so reluctant to move in toward the stage that I would start pointing at the audience, singling people out, waving for them to move in closer. In desperation, I've even jumped down to the dance floor myself to pull people up. Okay, so I broke my heel doing this and still suffer the consequences, but it worked. Don't break your foot, but do whatever you can to build up the dance floor, and then protect it with your life.

Transitions Between Musicians

No matter how hard you work to close the gap of death, it's easy to lose the audience between songs. As mentioned earlier, one surefire trick is to have the whole band move to the edge of the stage a few measures before the song ends. Engage the dance floor, lock eyes with people and smile at them—this will cause the crowd to stay with you because they'll be anticipating what's happening next.

When the first tune ends and the next one begins, stay up front, locked with the audience. If you're the one singing, move into the next song right away. If you're handing the baton to someone else, move to the side a bit and let the next person take the spotlight. The singer is already center stage with the rest of the band, so the transition is seamless. When people start dancing to the new song's groove, you know that you've secured the dance floor. Only then should the rest of the band slowly back away from the edge and give the space to the front person. Repeat with each transition, and you'll keep that crowd engaged with you all night long.

Take Responsibility for the Show

If someone hands you a dance floor with ten people on it, it's your responsibility to pass it on to the next performer with ten or more still dancing. If you lose your audience throughout your performance and then hand off the dance floor with only two remaining, that's not cool. You have to ask yourself what went wrong during the performance to have lost eight out of ten people. If you're the only one singing or if you're singing two songs in a row, you want to be conscious of adding to the dance floor from song to song—not losing people during each new tune.

You might think, *How is that my fault? It was the song or this and that.* Wrong. Take responsibility for the dance floor. Own it. Every person in the band must see it as his or her responsibility to keep the energy up and to avoid the gap of death. Creating a culture of never losing the dance floor is crucial.

Here's a mantra to repeat every time you take the stage: *It's my show.* It's your responsibility to make every night Saturday night.

Make the Right Moves

When you're onstage, you need to move to the music and make your performance something worth watching. That doesn't mean acting out the lyrics—clutching your heart or draping your hand across your forehead while you sing, "At first, I was afraid; I was petrified..." Don't raise your arms or look to the imaginary sun as you sing, "I see the sun rising" or point to your heart and then to the audience when you sing, "I love you." This isn't musical theater. It's not that kind of gig.

Some musicians act out the lyrics because they know that they need to move air, but they feel awkward doing so and don't know what to do with their bodies. Others move their lips, silently singing the songs along with the lead singer. Don't. If you're not singing, you shouldn't act as if you are.

Here are some moves to practice during rehearsals so that you don't end up looking like a dud during your next performance:

- **Feel it**: Really feel the emotion behind the words and show it in your facial expressions.

- **Sway**: When in doubt, sway. When there is no predetermined choreography, have the band sway from left to right starting on the "one." Why the left and not the right? Why not? You have to pick a side.

- **Get down**: Don't overwork or overdo this one, but falling to your knees during your guitar solo or when it's your time to shine shows the audience you're having a love affair with the music.

- **Kick**: Don't get violent, but unleash a kick or two to emphasize the last note or a huge punch in the music. Again, feel the music or it will look forced or tacky.

- **Spin**: Obviously, you don't want to get tangled in your wires, but otherwise, go nuts and spin in place or all the way across the stage.

- **Jump**: When you want the crowd to really go crazy, jump around. This creates high-energy excitement that really draws everyone into the action onstage.

- **Switch places**: Have the guitar and bass players walk to the opposite sides of the stage. Or have the singer switch places with the guitar player. Make sure that you practice these moves during rehearsals. Switching places looks really cool onstage.

- **Engage**: Sing and play straight to the audience and connect with some of your guests by giving them high fives or fist bumps. Who doesn't love that shit?

- **Get organized**: If you can get even the smallest amount of choreography down during your rehearsals—a sway here, a raised arm there, or together lean forward or lean back—you'll be miles ahead of other bands. Remember: people are not only listening; they're watching you too. Give them a show.

- **Reach the edge**: Get right up to the edge of the stage. If most of the band members can do this, it'll create that party vibe and invite everyone in the audience to join in. It also forces the audience to pay attention, which is very important during transitions.

- **Move**: Here's the main takeaway: don't stand in one place. Remember your place, but move around so you never look or seem passive or "Velcroed" to your spot onstage. Even if the stage is really small and you have one square foot, you can still move in your little space.

Whatever you do, don't pull one of these moves out for the first time during a performance. Respect the stage enough to rehearse before you try it in a show.

Don't Be Afraid to Be a Little Naughty

Remember, this is show business. Think Lady Gaga. Think Madonna. Think Prince. Make sure you apply the right behavior to the right venue, but push the envelope a little. The guys in my band sometimes play with their shirts off; the girls wear see-through clothing purposely displaying decorative and fancy push-up bras. If there's a bachelorette party in the audience and you're a guy and everyone is in a playful mood, bring the bride-to-be onstage, sprinkle salt on your neck, and let her have a go and follow it up with a tequila shot—yes, we did that, and they lost their minds! Nobody forgets crazy, fun shit like that, certainly not the bride-to-be. Do what you find fun and feel comfortable with. If you're not comfortable with being that naughty, don't do it; just don't be boring.

Feed Off Each Other's Energy

During any given song, glance at your bandmates and see who's feeling the music. Whether it's the drummer or singer, walk up to that person and feel the music together—eye to eye, not just shoulder to shoulder. Don't be fake about this connection. Don't paste on a huge fake smile or stiffly turn your head to look at the drummer. Do it in a way that is authentic and meaningful.

Something happens when band members look at each other and feed off each other's energy. When one person is grooving and the other person sees it and feels it, they lock in that groove. When the band is engaged at a high level, that shared energy is contagious and makes it impossible for the crowd not to be wowed and drawn in.

When You Are Singing, Take the Spotlight

There's nothing more off-putting than going out of your way to seem humble when you should be taking the spotlight. If it's your turn to sing, man, take the stage! Own it. At that moment you are the star, so rock it.

Play the Song, Not the Instrument

Some musicians like to go onstage and add licks and fills just for the sake of playing stuff, without stopping to think about what is appropriate to the song and to the music as a whole. Those musicians are not playing the song. They're playing the instrument.

When musicians overplay a song, they're acting as if the song is there to serve them, that its only purpose is to allow them to express themselves in whatever way they see fit. Nothing is further from the truth. Musicians are there to serve the tune, not the other way around. Think about Michael Jackson's "Beat It." That song needs a straight solid groove from all the instruments, from beginning to end. Nothing else.

Overplaying is a disease among musicians, and it is contagious. One person may play a lick, and another looks over and gives a thumbs up, and the next does the same. If a song has four notes and a guitarist knows he can play thirty, he'll try to fit them. Then the bass player might join in and try to insert the fill he just learned. Everyone onstage is so proud of this back-and-forth athletic musical exchange.

Meanwhile, the song has totally changed, and the audience has no clue what song they are listening to anymore.

Think of it like this: if every musician in your band added just one note to their part, congratulations, you just wrote a whole new song! In pop music especially, the difference between one song and the next can be a single note—a sixteenth note on the kick drum instead of an eighth.

In general, the best way to make sure that you're playing the song is to *play the song*, exactly as the original artist did. The tune sold millions of copies as is for a reason. If the band or a producer wanted to add a lick or a cowbell, they would have added them in the first place. They've already thought through the whole tune, every note and every detail, and put it out to the world. Obviously, it works exactly as is. Come on—who's going to show up with a better version of "What's Going On?" by Marvin Gaye?

When musicians or singers show up to rehearsal with their own version and enhancements to a melody or to a bass line, it's often because they didn't take time to learn the original tune, and they're hiding behind claims like, "I'm just doing my thing, man. I can't be stifled here." Adding your own bits like this is detrimental to the tune. It can throw off your bandmates since your changes affect their parts.

Learn the tune exactly as it is. Nail the atmosphere, the essence of the lyrics, and the feel. Do it justice out of respect for the original artist. That should always be the starting point. If you do that, you can also ask yourselves, "Do we want to do something unique with this tune? Is it even necessary? Should we take some liberties with the melody or the rhythm section, insert a solo or a rap, mix it with another tune, let the intro vamp for a while, play it as a bossa nova...?" Ultimately, you want to ask yourselves, "If we did X, would the tune be more exciting?"

If the answer is no, and 80 percent of the time it will be, don't touch it. Period. Remember, you're serving your audience, and they find it very annoying when you change tunes that they know by heart. However, if your changes make the tune more exciting without overdoing it, then knock yourself out and have some fun. But it should be an arrangement, intelligently thought through and practiced during rehearsal, and never a free for all.

When the main concern is the tune itself, you will always know when you are over- or underplaying. Once musicians stop focusing on themselves, they will always know what kind of feeling they are delivering to the crowd.

Don't Visit Too Long

Some musicians like to go into the audience during a song and walk around. That's fine, as long as they don't overdo it. Spend a minute or two on the floor, and then get back up onstage.

The problem with walking amid the crowd is that most people can't see you, but they'll keep searching, which moves their attention away from the band. This is where you might start losing the show. If you want to mingle with the crowd, keep it very brief. You might create a showstopper here, and then get right back onstage and reconnect with the entire audience and your bandmates. This creates a great atmosphere for everyone.

Tension and Release

An exciting performance involves a constant back and forth of tension and release. When you build tension, you grab the audience's attention and steadily increase their expectation that something exciting is about to happen. Once the momentum is built, that's when you break that tension and give them that special "something."

One way to add tension is to do what we call a band freeze. Get into the groove of the song, pump up the sound, and then suddenly stop playing and freeze in place— singer holding mic to lips, drummer with sticks hovering above the drum set, guitarist with hands on the strings. This startles the room and brings everyone into a laser-point focus on what's happening onstage. Tension builds as everyone anxiously waits. Then on cue, the whole band kicks in again, releasing and yet building on the tension, and the crowd goes ape-shit.

Another way to add tension is to have the whole band walk forward at the same time, play at the edge of the stage, and then walk back together. Or try playing an intense, rockin' tune, followed by a lighthearted reggae song, or three intense songs followed by something mellow. The key is to keep the pattern going: tension, release; tension, release.

Don't Drink Too Much

If you're playing in a bar, some of you will drink; that's just the way it is. But don't drink to the point where it affects your performance. Remember why you're there: to give the audience a performance that they won't forget, not drunken chaos. Alcohol tends to be a big problem among musicians, so know thyself. Every major disaster that's happened with many of our bands was related to alcohol: singing off-key, forgetting parts, getting paranoid and lashing out, playing very loud, not being able to keep their balance, beating each other up, picking fights with the audience, not being able to finish the show, not showing up at all, you name it. Don't blow your career and all of your hard work by drinking too much. A bad reputation is hard to fix.

Take Breaks When Drinks Are Full

As you look around the room during your performance, take note of the tables. Are they filled with empty glasses? If so, people might be getting ready to leave, but you may get them to stay a while longer by playing a couple more songs and then by saying something inviting like, "Hey, beautiful people, why don't you get a few more drinks?

We're not going anywhere," and then take a break yourselves. Now people are more likely to stay because they
had a chance to hang out with you between sets and they
have some new drinks. Because you managed to charm
your audience into staying, you now have a bigger crowd
for your last set, which is a lot more fun than an empty
place. Plus, the bar owner has made more money.

If you're on a tight schedule with the bar, taking breaks
when drinks are full might be more difficult. As you build
a relationship with the owner and staff, you might try to
reach an agreement with the owner or manager to "bend"
those rules/schedule a little and to orchestrate this better.
In the end, it's to everyone's advantage.

Save Your Beef for the Brief

No matter how much you rehearse, shit happens during
a performance. The bass player misses a cue. The drummer doesn't bring in the band properly. Someone steps on
someone's shoes. The gap of death widens.

Yes, you need to get those problems out in the open,
but not onstage. Don't show your annoyance or anger in
the middle of a tune. It's done. You can't fix what's already
happened, and you want to make sure you give the audience your best during the entirety of the show.

In between sets, you want to bring up the issues that
you can actually fix so that the audience has a better experience. Usually these are small adjustments. For example,

if the gap of death widened on song three or the drummer got too loud at the end of song four or the band is getting passive, bring that up, so everyone is aware that they need to watch the gap and volume in the next set. But keep it positive. The goal isn't to criticize. You want to say it, get everyone to let it go, and then focus on bringing your best for the rest of the gig.

As for the rest of the issues related to missed cues or sloppy dance moves, take notes about what happened, but save your beef for the brief, preferably at the next meeting or rehearsal where you do a brief on all the points that need cleaning up. You won't be playing those songs again that night, so there's no reason to waste energy talking about them now. Just focus on bringing the best experience to the audience in front of you.

Huddle Between Sets

While you don't want to fix major issues between sets, you do want to prepare for what's coming up. If you know that you've somehow lost the dance floor the last time that you played two of the songs in the second, third or fourth set, that's what you bring up. You can say, "Look, guys. These songs are coming up again, and we know what happened last time. Tonight, come hell or high water, we're going to have a full dance floor by song three."

These mid-show briefs are perfect for giving small, specific goals to your band members and getting everyone to refocus and reset. It's your opportunity to have each person approach the next set with a clear understanding of what their mission is.

To make the most of these huddles, you have to be aware of what's happening onstage and in the audience. You might see some people you know standing in the back of the club, or you might sense the energy from a certain table and realize they're either ready to party or ready to leave. During the briefs, you can say, "Hey, make sure to say hi to Mo and Richard," or "Focus on those girls at table two. They're ready to explode, so light them up."

Once you scan the room, you'll start to see who your party-starters are. You'll know who will start a chain reaction and fill the dance floor. Once you see it, take time during the break to strategize with the band on how to crank up the energy by having them focus on a certain group.

At the beginning, this may seem difficult to practice because it has to be done in real time, on location. You don't have an audience in your rehearsal room and can't anticipate what kind of people will be at the gig. With experience you'll find the same scenarios happening over and over again. You may have different faces in the audience, but you'll see the same overall behaviors, so you'll be able to anticipate pitfalls and general strategies. Still, the real experience comes from being responsive at the show. You should be aware that you have a group of party-starters in the audience and step it up so that your band members become *the* party-starters.

If you're like me, having a bad set will really bum you out and give you a knot in your stomach that won't go away. Regardless, the briefs are the time to give mini pep talks, not long-winded corrections. It's like praying before a meal or meeting in a huddle before each play in a football game—important, but short and to the point.

Surprise the Crowd

Sometimes when we came back from a break, we'd have everyone except the drummer stay offstage. Then the crowd would hear sounds from people who weren't actually in front of them. The guitarist would walk in from the back and the singer would come in from the side, and the crowd would eat it up.

Other times we would all wear dress clothes for sets one and two, and then we'd come out in jeans and T-shirts for set three. One time I sang an Arabic song, and a Lebanese percussionist joined us onstage. Another time we had belly dancers go through the audience. If I knew that one table had a bunch of Latin ladies, I'd say something like, "When we play this next tune, I know the Latin ladies are gonna bring it!"

Little surprises like these put a smile on people's faces. Even if you're a wonderful band, your show can get monotonous for repeat customers. If you keep people excited and having fun, they'll keep coming back.

Showstoppers

Every show needs special elements, and this is more than just hitting all your notes. You can rehearse all you want, know a thousand songs, and still have a boring show. It doesn't matter that you're laying it all out if the audience isn't picking it up. You should always have showstoppers to grab people's attention and give them something to remember.

Have you ever watched *The Voice* or *American Idol*? When the singer hits that certain note, the camera pans to the judges and the crowd to show people in tears. That's a showstopper. Think about a crowd's response to Prince's "Purple Rain" or Tina Turner's "Proud Mary." Songs like those are guaranteed showstoppers (assuming that you play them well).

A showstopper gets people from clapping politely to screaming and losing their minds. It's what gets people shouting for more and telling their friends, "Oh my God, tomorrow, you have to come see this band with us. They're amazing!"

Showstoppers aren't just for frontmen either. Every member can get involved. I've had guitarists play on their knees and drummers go *crazy* playing a solo over a repetitive musical pattern. We used to do a tutti, where all of the instruments play a pattern that is usually very fast and musically very difficult, like a solo but everyone plays the same notes at the same time. Imagine five musicians all playing the solo from "Hotel California" with the exact same notes at the exact same time. It was extremely difficult to pull off, but people loved it big time. It was very effective and memorable.

In one of my first showstoppers, I rapped like Eminem. I got so close to the original version that people thought it was pre-recorded and I was lip-syncing. So one day to prove myself, I stopped the band and kept rapping solo for sixteen measures. When the band came back in, the audience went crazy.

When I saw how well that worked, we made the Eminem section part of the show. Then we started experimenting. We mixed "Kashmir" from Led Zeppelin with "Lose Yourself" from Eminem. At one point, two super-talented alpha members of my band, LA and Kolette, were not getting along. They were both like sisters to me, and I didn't want to let either one go, so I decided to make a show out of their antagonistic relationship. We worked out the whole routine ahead of time. I would dance super closely with Kolette in an extremely sensual way, and then LA would storm in dancing, with an angry look, and pull me away, dancing even closer to me. This went back and forth with the drama building. No one smiled or giggled. It was intense and magical, and people came back in droves. We packed that place out and broke the sales record more times than I can remember.

Like anything else in your performance, showstoppers should be thought through. What works for one song doesn't guarantee that it will work for another, so you have to practice it. Find ways to create the tension that makes people pay attention. It could be that the whole band pauses or you all do the splits on a certain note. During an interlude of one of our showstopper songs, one of our musicians would grab our lead singer, tango, and dip her to within a centimeter of the floor. It was crazy and exciting, and the crowd used to wait for it to happen. Give people something to remember the next day. Otherwise, it's just another song and just another band. You might as well put on a CD.

When planning a set, you plan showstoppers along with your A+, A, B, and C songs in the same W pattern. Put your showstoppers at the peaks, where most of the energy is. If you have A+ songs that aren't showstoppers, put them just before the showstoppers, right under the peaks. Now you've rejuvenated the entire set. Remember the point isn't that the peaks are exciting and the valleys are boring. No part of your show should ever be boring. These peaks and valleys are another way to create tension and release. People can't be hollering for forty-five minutes straight. So you give them a release. You play a ballad. They're still engaged and drawn in, maybe even crying or having goosebumps, but it's all a release from the tension you've carefully built up.

You might be wondering, what's the difference between an A+ song and a showstopper? An A+ song is exciting and creates a wonderful atmosphere. People will walk away saying, "I like that band." A showstopper burns the memory of your band and that night into their brains. When I go on tours to check our bands, people who had seen me onstage years earlier come up to me and remind me of everything we did onstage. They still remembcred, years and years later.

Never tell yourself it's just a cover band and you're just playing in a bar. You can be far more impactful than you think.

Draw an Encore

You can also use a showstopper to draw an encore at the end of each show. When you finish, leave a small hint that you might come back. You could leave the lights on, keep a hum going from the keyboard, anything you can think of to get the crowd wondering if something is going to happen.

You can also tease the audience by saying something like, "I guess it's time to go home," inviting the crowd to scream, "Noooo!"

"Yes, yes, time to go home. Nothing to see here."

"Nooooooo!"

"But guys, you have jobs to go to. Traffic to be stuck in tomorrow. Who would want another drink and some more fun, would youuuuuu?"

"Yeahhhhh!"

Then the drums come in with a thunder and wham, and off you go.

If you come back with a killer encore, people will come back again and again and again, and the bar owner will pay you a lot more than any other band, guaranteed.

Show the Staff Some Love Too

While you're keeping the crowd entertained, the servers and bartenders are working double-time to quench everyone's thirst. Before the show ends, acknowledge them by saying something like, "Hey, ladies and gentlemen, don't forget to thank and tip your wonderful staff. They've been on their feet all night, and they've been doing a fantastic job." Staff all over the world have thanked me for this little shout-out, because people do tip them more as a result.

Practice the Walk-Off

Equally important is how you walk off the stage. By this time, you will be sweaty, exhausted, and exhilarated, feeling a sense of accomplishment and joy because you left it all onstage. After the last song, have the drummer stand up and all of the musicians walk over to the edge of the stage and take a bow. Have the front person say, "Thank you, ladies and gentlemen, you've been wonderful tonight." Let the audience roar, then cut the lights, quietly set down your instruments, and walk off the stage in the dark, single file. Leave people knowing without a doubt that you gave everything and left all that you have out there on the stage, just for them. This shows true professionalism.

Pack Up and Clean Your Stage

Whatever you do, don't finish the last tune and start cleaning and packing up while all eyes are still on stage. It looks like you can't wait to get the hell out of there. Instead, walk off professionally, and when eyes are no longer on the stage, come back and discreetly start cleaning up. Take your beer or soda glass to the bar. Nothing pisses off bar owners and staff more than cleaning after the musicians. It's a simple matter of courtesy; they serve you drinks throughout the evening, the least you can do is to clean up after yourselves. This simple act will set you apart from other bands that don't think about doing so. Remember to remain a class act at all times.

Once the stage is clean, spend a few minutes on the floor, thank a few customers, and if you are ready to leave, pack up quietly and head out. Don't say, "Hey, I'm leaving," because the audience may take that as an indirect way of saying they should leave as well. For the bar owner's sake, don't make a big deal of leaving, so people know they can hang out and have another drink.

Leave Together

When you're all cleaned up and it's time to leave, tell the band it's time to go. Or at least make sure that as the band leader, you're the last one out. If you don't, you're setting yourself up for many problems that happen after the boss leaves and the band lets loose: they overdrink, hit on the wrong person, freeload off customers, and more.

It's best to come in together professionally and exit the same way, with the band leader saying the last goodbye— at least until the band values are internalized and consistently lived out by every musician. If the band is trained, you can just chill as the leader, but if the band is new and the values are not truly clear yet, don't take any chances because the next gig may not be there.

Take Notes

So the show wasn't that great. Take notes as soon as you can, and encourage everyone else to do the same. Don't wait until the end of the night; you'll never remember all the little things that happened throughout the performance. Whenever something comes up during the show, jot down a note on the set list or form right after the set. If the audience loses interest when you play "Single Ladies," write "lost audience" next to that song. If there was a mistake in the song structure, write "fix bridge" or "practice ending" on the form. Also, write all the miscellaneous stuff like "so-and-so kept looking at his watch" or "so-and-so was distracted during set two." Just write a simple note that will trigger your memory of what happened.

At the next rehearsal, go over every member's notes so that you can analyze them and make all the necessary adjustments to get your show to a near flawless level. If you've tried a song several times but it's just a dud, throw it out! Or if a song has gone really well several times, develop it into a showstopper.

This simple practice of taking short notes while performing can help you tremendously in refining your show.

Lots of bands won't take the time to do this. They'll simply walk up onstage and blindly do the same thing they did the day before. Those bands won't get the benefit of learning from their mistakes and the chance to keep growing. Not very inspiring to be in bands like that.

Improve Weekly

Using the information gained from each show, make it your goal to improve at least one aspect of your performance every rehearsal. If you improve one stance, one groove, one smile at a time by even 1 percent, think of how much better you'll be in a month or a year.

When you focus on improvement and delighting the audience, everyone stays motivated and focused. There's no time to be bored or passive, and there's no time to bicker or complain because you're so engaged in doing what you love with people that you love for the audience that you love. Isn't that what we all want?

That said, many musicians have not been coached or given regular feedback to help them improve, unlike athletes who often seek it out. As a result, many musicians get offended easily when they receive constructive feedback. They don't want to be coached on presentation, wardrobe, or dance moves. My suggestion: create a culture of feedback, where it is given and received regularly—after sets, gigs, rehearsals. After a while, it will become what you do as a band, and the musicians will actually seek it out as part of their effort to improve their skills and the show as a whole. Once you work like this on a regular basis, you will never last a minute in a complacent band.

IT'S ALL ABOUT THE AUDIENCE

Most musicians feel like life started when they picked up an instrument and that playing onstage is what they were meant to do. If you respect the stage and keep it sacred, you can show the audience that what you do is incredibly special. You can alter their mood and create a shared experience they will remember for years to come. Music can touch people at the deepest level, and you have the amazing opportunity to be a part of that.

The stage is where the audience gets to know you as a performer. The floor is where they get to know you as a person. That track is up next.

ISOLATE YOURSELF

Before you walk onstage before your next show, isolate yourself for five to ten minutes. Decide in your mind's eye how you are going to walk out onstage, what you want the feeling onstage to be, the exact facial expressions you want to see on your fellow musicians. See yourself performing set one, beginning to end, and then sets two and three and so on. Picture what the crowd will be doing, the looks on their faces, their body language, what you will do if they seem too laid-back or passive, or even bored. Picture the staff walking around serving drinks and the mood they're in.

Let that vision live in your head for a good moment, and then walk onstage and create it.

The more you do that, before every show in every bar in every city, the more consistently you will be able to create that reality every night. You will be 100 percent certain that you can deliver on your promise to a bar owner that when your band plays, every night is Saturday night.

Write your pre-gig ritual, share on social media, and tag me with #stagetime #gigforlife.

FLOOR TIME

I n 2000, my friend Steve Radcliffe landed a job as the food and beverage director at the Grand Hyatt Erawan in Bangkok—a very coveted position. Soon after, he hired my band, Shades, to play at Spasso, an Italian restaurant by day and packed nightclub by night situated on the lower floor of the Grand Hyatt.

Spasso had a dance floor in the middle of a half circle, which was full of tables when the restaurant was open. When the dinner rush ended, the staff cleared the tables to make room for the evening crowd.

Soon after we started gigging there, I started dreaming of how I was going to pack that floor, because Spasso was *the* place to play in Bangkok. I wanted to play there as much as possible, and drawing in people who bought drinks was my ticket.

I started by meeting with the managers and asking for a floor plan of the bar. I wanted to see the number of tables, and I wanted to see the sales totals every night. They thought I was crazy. "Georges, we don't share that information," they told me.

"Oh, you're going to share it with me," I replied. "You have to."

"Why do we have to?"

"Because you're judging my performance and whether I'll be asked back based on sales. If you don't share that information, how do I know if I'm winning or losing?"

They couldn't argue with that logic, and they gave me what I asked for. Armed with that information, we went to work. Within six weeks, we had broken the nightly sales record in a club that had been open for eighteen years.

How did we do this? By creating a system for floor time that drew crowds back night after night.

Floor time is about creating a meaningful relationship with the audience as human beings first and foremost. Unfortunately, this is the most ignored aspect of building a band. What happens instead is that bands fall into a boring routine of welcoming the audience from the stage, playing their tunes from the stage, and thanking the audience from the stage before they walk off the stage and head out. When they're done playing, most musicians pack their shit and leave the club as if a fire alarm went off, which leaves the customers feeling neglected.

They would've simply enjoyed shaking the band members' hands and thanking them for a memorable evening.

If you want to build a following, you have to remember that those are human beings out there, listening to you play, dancing to your tunes, clapping their hands, and smiling at you. Invest time and energy in connecting with the people who pay so you can play.

WHOSE CUSTOMERS ARE THEY?

This is the golden question, and one that you must keep in the back of your mind at all times when you think about floor time. It's actually a trick question. These people were your *audience* when you were on stage, but they've always been the bar's *customers*. Even if your friends or significant others come to watch you play, as soon as they walk in, they are now the bar's customers. These people have simply been entrusted into your custody for a few hours on any given evening. Handle with care.

When you walk onto the floor between sets and after the show, be friendly, engaging, and personable. But always remember: they are not your customers.

NOT YOUR JOB

Because customers develop a relationship with you, they will sometimes come to you with complaints about the bartender or the service. They might even ask you to talk to the bar owner. Don't do it. Remember, they are not your customers, and that means problems with the bar staff or service are not yours to solve. Listen politely, empathize, ask if they've talked to the manager, but that's it. Stay out of it.

Don't Look Desperate

There's a fine line between being engaged and looking desperate. Try, but don't try too hard. When the set is finished, don't race out to the dance floor. That just looks desperate, man, as if getting attention onstage for the last few hours wasn't enough.

When you finish the set, put your instruments down and walk off professionally. Then give it a minute. If you're doing a brief with your band, that gives you a natural buffer, a pause so that you don't look too eager, but don't wait too long, or they'll be gone. We're talking two minutes, max. Then go mingle with the crowd, but not on the dance floor. The show is over.

Another thing that can make you look desperate is drinking too much after the show. When people get drunk, they say the dumbest shit. Depending on what you say, you'll be judged and labeled, and your reputation could be destroyed by a single drunken interaction. I'm not saying that you have to drink water all night. Have a drink, maybe two depending on your tolerance, but don't kid yourself. You always have to be in control and show professionalism.

Also, make sure that you're not the last one to leave the bar. The staff are tired and they want to go home. By hanging around with that one last customer you are delaying their schedules and their lives, and they will become resentful—and rightly so.

Pay Serious Attention to Hygiene

Nightclubs and bars are an intimate setting, and live music brings a sexy energy. People are very loose. You wouldn't go to the grocery store and kiss the cashier, but it's common for girls to kiss and hug a band member. If they approach you for a hug or a kiss, it would be to your benefit to smell great, despite having sweat buckets during your performance. If they smell popcorn, peanuts, beer, and cigarettes, that's a nasty turnoff. Pack some mint spray or a toothbrush and some toothpaste in your hygiene bag.

Notice how I did not say to pack some gum in your hygiene bag. Gum is a big no-no. Never chew gum on or off-stage. It makes you look like a twelve-year-old who dressed as a rock star for Halloween.

Performing live music is a sweaty business, which means body odor is always a possibility. Before you start hugging and kissing fans, you better smell good regardless of your fashion or performing style; you can look messy and sweaty, be wearing ripped jeans, baggy pants and a T-shirt, and even covered in tattoos. No matter what, you still need to be clean and smell fresh. Believe it or not, my bands have gotten many, many complaints about body odor over the years, and it's embarrassing feedback. Don't be the stinker.

Before we went out into the crowd, my bandmates and I used to hug each other and do a smell check—yes, a smell check. I would rather hear from my friend that I smell funky, and take care of it right away, than have someone in the audience say, "Talented cat, but daaamn!"

Accept Compliments

Let's say you go out into the crowd between sets and someone says, "Great job!" or "You guys sound fantastic!" No matter how you think you played, don't respond with something like "Oh, we sound like shit tonight," or "Ahh I'm so tired," or "My voice is shot." That kind of response ruins the experience for the person.

If the customer says you sound great and you say, "No, we sound like crap," you just insulted him. You basically told him he doesn't know what he's talking about. On the other hand, trying to act super humble when someone compliments you can have the opposite effect and make you seem obnoxious.

Your best bet is to simply accept the compliment. Say something like "Thank you so much. I'm glad you liked it.

Please enjoy the rest of the show." And leave it at that. It's their experience, and it's positive, so don't ruin it.

KEEP THE RELATIONSHIPS PROFESSIONAL

Say it with me: they are not your customers. They need to be treated professionally and with respect. Romantic relationships between band members and people in the audience happen all the time. It's the norm. But they have to be handled with care so you don't jeopardize your chance of rebooking a gig at that club.

When you're a musician, you have to keep all relationships professional when you're in the club—even those with your significant others.

Romantic Relationships

At some point, you and your band members will get into romantic relationships with audience members, but you have to tread lightly, especially when you're new to the bar. Don't be too eager. You don't know which staff member might be dating which guest—or if they used to date and had a horrible breakup, or if they are just plain psycho. You have to be careful who you hook up with.

My band and I traveled to Surabaya, Indonesia, for a four-month contract. We had a rule: no hooking up with audience members for the first three weeks of the gig, so you can figure out who's who. Well, the day after our first show, one of my bandmates came knocking on my door with a flustered look on his face and asked for help. He said, "There's a woman trying to kill herself in my washroom!"

"What! What the hell are you talking about?"

Apparently, he had picked up some woman at the show, brought her to his room, and then when he asked her to leave, she refused. Then she started freaking out, locked herself up in the washroom, and told him that she wanted to take her life and was ready to take a pack of pills. It was very traumatic. We had to call security and have her dragged out. It turned out that she was bluffing; she just didn't want to leave. The pills she threatened to pop were multivitamins. Now it makes me laugh, but it wasn't funny at the time. We had only been there for forty-eight hours when all of this drama unfolded that could have gotten us fired.

Another time one of the musicians unknowingly hooked up with an ambassador's wife. Somehow the general manager found out and told me, "Georges, he is going to get killed." So we had him on a plane within an hour.

When you go to a bar, don't do anything stupid. Just have a couple of drinks and keep a good head on your shoulders. Don't get caught up in the current of men or women who want you—and there will be truck loads. The bar owners are watching you. The staff are watching you. The audience is watching you. They all want to know if you're there to play music or to mess around. If the manager or owner sees someone in your band who is primarily on the hunt, you're probably not going to get invited back.

Friendships

Another rule of thumb: keep friendships in the club. Romantic relationships happen, but if a customer invites you out for dinner or for a spin on the ocean in their yacht, politely decline. If you don't, you're going to run into problems. Why? Because that customer will no doubt feel entitled to special treatment, be it being singled out and thanked from the stage for coming to every performance, or only joining their table between sets. They'll be in your business the second you step off the stage, which will keep you from working the room and building community with all of your fans. They'll start sharing their opinions about other members of the band. Things escalate, and it just gets really complicated.

Even if you honor floor time and keep friendships in the club, it's easy to get stuck at one table. Don't Velcro the customers like that. It may not feel like you're "stuck"—you could be having the time of your life—but there's a time and a place for fun. Just like stage time, floor time is business time; it's not a break to rest between sets. You're on the clock. You should be focused on the audience from the time you step into the club until the time you leave. If you're not mingling with your fans, getting them to stay longer, and inviting them to the next show, you're not doing your job.

Significant Others

Let's say your significant other wants to come to the show, as is the norm for all of us. Remember this: while they're in the crowd, you have to treat them like every other person in the crowd. They can't put extra demands on your time and keep you from building other relationships. If your special someone can't handle that, then they should stay home.

There is no other job in the world where your partner can come into your office to hang out with you or sit on your lap while you're at work. Imagine doing that if you worked at a bank or a law firm. No way; it would never happen.

People always say, "Yoko Ono broke up the Beatles." No, John Lennon broke up the Beatles because he broke a major rule. Instead of saying, "Sorry, babe, we're working here. This isn't your band, and you are not a musician. You're in the way, and you're not contributing. Having you here is a pain in the ass for the rest of the band because they can't be themselves"—he allowed Yoko to be at every rehearsal, every gig, every meeting. In one documentary on the Beatles, you see Yoko sitting in the fifth chair in every single scene: painting her nails, eating lunch, fidgeting, flipping pages, emotionless, disconnected, being totally indifferent—what a turnoff. She had no business being there. John should have kept that nutcase as far as possible from his workspace.

MANAGE THE AUDIENCE

So far, I have spent twenty-six years of my life in beautiful Asia, staying at amazing hotels. The second time that I returned to one of those hotels in Hong Kong, the doorman greeted me by name when I walked in the door. The bellhop at the elevator knew my name. The housekeeper and bartender knew my name. They had a fantastic fruit plate waiting for me in the room. The staff must have observed which fruit I ate and which I ignored because the next morning, the fruit plate had more of the fruit I had eaten the previous morning. Every person who worked at this hotel made sure I had a special, personalized experience. Because they paid so much attention to the details and my preferences, the staff made me feel like a VIP and the whole experience has remained engraved in my mind for years.

During floor time, you should put in the same effort to get to know your audience. Don't interrogate people; just ask a few questions as a matter of natural conversation. Learn people's names. Learn their kids' names. Find out what they do for a living and what they drink. Ask their favorite song. Make them feel special. Everyone in your audience—as a matter of fact, every person in your life—will be a stranger at first, but it only takes a handshake to turn them into someone you know.

To make sure that my band and I did this consistently and systematically, I developed a system for managing the audience and creating a community.

Break Up the Room

Once you start getting repeat gigs at the same venue, pay attention to the room's layout. Then divide up the room and fan out between sets. Have each musician take a section of tables and go greet the people in that section. Within a few minutes, you can meet every person in the room and thank them for coming. Everyone feels special, their presence acknowledged, and they'll want to come back.

As this becomes a habit for you, night after night, you'll start developing more insight that will help you improve your floor time immensely. Pay attention to which sections fill up and which ones don't, which sections tend to buy the most drinks, and which ones tend to flood the dance floor.

Some performers might argue that if you're breaking up or sectioning the audience like that, then you run the risk of not treating everyone equally. Yeah, that's the whole point. Every member of your audience is going to need or want to be treated differently.

You'll learn that some people bring more energy, and some need more enticement. By breaking up the room into sections, you and your bandmates gain all of these insights, which will help you make connections and build your community. Your fans will stay longer, come back more often, pack the room, drink more, and create a superb atmosphere.

As you meet and greet around the club, some of you may get harassed here and there. Shit happens when there's alcohol involved, so be prepared. Your pretty singers may get a tap on the bum as they walk by a table; your handsome guys may have women hug them hard or kiss them on the cheek and even stain their white shirts with makeup.

Should such incidents occur, don't take matters into your own hands, because you may say or do something that you might regret and make matters worse. If you happen to be the band leader, go straight to the venue's management and let them handle those awkward situations. And tell your band members to come straight to you.

Also, if you notice that guests at a certain table have had a bit too much to drink and are becoming unruly and out of control, feel free to avoid those folks when you break up the room. While you do want to form relationships with everyone in the audience, you also have to be smart. One night a gentleman almost broke my lead singer's fingers when he shook her hand because he was so drunk that he didn't realize how hard he was squeezing. When she managed to pull away, she was in tears. Needless to say, we avoided his table for the rest of the night.

WHO DO YOU GREET FIRST?

When you meet a couple out on the floor, things can get a little funky. If you happen to be the male musician in this scenario, stay on the safe side and always greet the guy first. Once you feel that the vibe is cool, extend your hand and greet his lady. The same applies if you're a female singer or musician: always greet the woman first. If the girlfriend is the jealous type, she might rip your eyes out if she thinks you're getting too friendly with her man.

Drunk people in bars can get feisty. If they think you're hitting on their guy or girl, it can get messy. If you're a guy, turn your attention back to the guy after you greet his girl—unless you want to get punched in the face; the same if the situation is switched. Seriously, these things happen often. Even if you greet the guy first, he might watch what you do with your eyes. Are you checking out his girl's legs? Remember where you are and why you're talking to them. Get in, greet, get out, and go meet other customers.

Make Audience Profiles

During the first couple of weeks on a gig, it's hard to get used to the rhythm of the crowd. Pretty quickly, though, you'll discover who the regulars are. Once you get familiar with your audience, they become your people. You don't need a million people to be successful. You just need to build genuinely respectful relationships with the people who do attend, and guaranteed, you'll end up with a grateful fan base that genuinely supports you.

As you meet and greet throughout the evening, think about your approach and what things you're going to say. Take mental notes and create a profile for each person that you meet: their names, their partners' names, the songs that they loved, those that they didn't, what they like to drink, and so on. Jot down this information away from the fans, or after the set while it's still fresh in your mind. This exercise may seem awkward at first, but in no time you'll notice just how impressed your guests will be when you shake hands and greet them by name, or give them a shoutout as you dedicate their favorite song to them or to their date. That's when you'll know that you're on the right path of creating relationships as you build an adoring fan base.

STAND UP

Whenever you meet someone and you happen to be sitting down, stand up before you shake their hand. Management, staff, and guests alike notice gestures like this. By standing up, you clearly show that you have class and that you're respectful.

You will never offend anyone by standing up to greet them, but you could lose a gig if you don't.

Introduce People

Once I learn customers' names, I introduce them to as many of the band members as I can between sets. Then I introduce guests to each other. For example, if a regular guest greets me on the floor and I happen to see someone else I've met, I'll say, "Hey, Roy, have you met Patrick? Patrick, come here, bro. This is Roy, a friend of mine and a great supporter of our band. I have to go back onstage. See you gents during the next break." And there you have it; networking at its best.

I'm Lebanese and an extrovert, so this kind of behavior is part of my culture and comes to me naturally, but that's not the case for everyone. My friend Marc was very friendly but shy, so I would bring him along when I went out into the crowd. If you happen to be the more extroverted one, ask one of the more introverted band members to join you to mingle with the crowd.

The more gigs you do, the more natural it will become. You'll recognize more faces, remember more names, and eventually, it'll feel like you know everyone. If you have two friends who haven't met, it will be the norm to introduce them to one another. It becomes the band's culture.

Once people start talking to each other, the band is under a lot less pressure. When Patrick comes back on Thursday and Roy's there with friends, it makes the venue seem less imposing, much more familiar, where people know him by name. He's now part of our community, and he feels that he belongs. Why would either of them go to any other club? (By the way, Patrick and Roy are real people and are still my friends today.)

Build Community

After you've introduced customers to one another, the atmosphere in the club will start buzzing with joy, laughter, friendships, and relationships in the making.

That community will grow on its own, almost on autopilot, but there are things that you can do to grow it and keep people coming back time after time.

MAKE EVERY NIGHT SATURDAY NIGHT

Killer band, fantastic atmosphere, full dance floor—that's what a Saturday night should look like. You turn your band into a killer band by getting it right during rehearsals. You create the atmosphere by focusing on the details: the lighting, the music, the showstoppers, the sound, the infectious interaction between the musicians onstage, the exchange of fun, and great vibes between the band and the audience. Then, you pack the club by getting to know the audience members at a more personal level. It is a systematic effort. It's what gets the crowds to stay, so that you can keep playing music for a living and gig for life.

REMEMBER, THEY'RE NOT YOUR CUSTOMERS

This one is worth repeating. In a way, it's liberating to remember that they're not your customers. During floor time, you can treat the bar like it's your friend's living room, and your job is to make sure that everyone in attendance at her party is having a superb evening. It's absolutely possible to have fun and stay professional at the same time.

KNOW YOUR ROLE

Your job is to entertain customers with your gift of musicianship. It's to make sure that everyone is happy. It's not to create gossip. It's not to make a drunken fool of yourself. Rock out all you want onstage, and keep the fun rolling when you're on the floor, too, but do it professionally and with class.

INVITE PEOPLE TO STICK AROUND

After you've chatted with a group of people, and you need to make your rounds, you can politely say something like, "Hey, man, it was great talking to you. I'm gonna go say hi to Dave and Phuong over there, but stick around: I want to have another drink with you before I head out." Make them feel special, so they want to stay for more.

TREAT THE CUSTOMERS

At some point, audience members are going to buy drinks for the band, and you're going to want to do the polite thing and pay them back. The problem is that buying drinks adds up real fast. Imagine having to buy drinks for three tables every night—you'd blow your pay for the night.

So I worked out a deal with the venue that allows the band to build community, buy drinks, and not go broke. The bar allows the band twenty free drinks per night that are designated to treat the customers. That way, if a band member is hanging out with a table that bought us drinks earlier in the evening, he can "buy" a round that will be charged to the venue instead of him. The musicians feel great, the audience members are touched, and people stick around and come back more often.

At cost price, the venue pays peanuts for those twenty drinks. Having the band buy audience members drinks is the cheapest retention program bar owners can use to keep the audience coming back. They basically gain a very effective PR team at little extra cost. Plus, it helps you build connections and community.

PAY GENUINE COMPLIMENTS

If there's a woman in the crowd who's looking lovely, I'm not afraid to just tell her, "You look beautiful today." If she just got highlights, I say, "Your highlights look amazing." You have no idea how many girls tell me, "Oh, my God, my husband didn't even notice!" I do it to guys too: "Hey, man, your haircut looks great." "Those are some nice shoes, bro; where'd you get those?"

Whatever you do, always make sure that your compliments are genuine; no one is ever offended by a genuine compliment. Don't say things that you don't mean. It's not cool, and people aren't stupid. They know the difference.

MAKE SOMEBODY HAPPY

As stated earlier, I did some soul searching recently in regard to why I do what I do, and I came to one conclusion: I want to make people happy. This is the purpose of my company, and it's what I expect from every band that I create. Making the crowd happy is what fueled me night after night when I was playing, and it still motivates me today. It's my compass, my north star. It keeps me going in the midst of the fatigue and setbacks. It's my raison d'être.

Making the crowd happy starts with making sure your band is happy. Your bandmates work so hard day in and day out, so once in a while when you notice that the energy is fizzling out, go get them each *one* tequila shot to kick off the next set with a good vibe. They don't drink? Give them hugs, thank them, hang out, go for walks together—it enriches your life and everyone else's.

Happiness is contagious, so if the band is happy, then the audience is too. If you make the waitress happy, she makes another table of customers happy. Tell a joke that spreads across the bar. Get people laughing. Happy people want to stay.

TREAT EVERYONE LIKE A VIP

If you treat everyone with respect—your audience, as well as suppliers, lenders, janitors, bartenders, housekeepers, musicians, venue owners—you will build solid relationships. This is what keeps people coming back to your shows, and they'll even bring some of their friends to experience the fun that they've been bragging about, growing the community of people that want to be around you and your band.

Be Discreet

If you have a longstanding relationship with a venue, you get to know the audience pretty well. Still, you have to remember that these people are not your customers, not your friends—not even your work colleagues. This is not the time to gossip. Whatever one customer tells you, assume it's in confidence and keep that information to yourself.

Confidentiality is extremely important, especially in nightclubs. People should feel like they're getting the best experience possible, not that they're being judged. If a customer asked me, "Hey, G, did you see how drunk Denise got last night?" I'd immediately say, "Honestly, man, I wasn't really paying attention, but I'm glad that she enjoyed herself." I'd leave it at that and change the subject. Of course, I saw how drunk Denise got; I'm not blind. I also saw how Frank showed up with his wife one night and his girlfriend the next (don't fool yourself; this shit happens the other way around, too, with women showing up with boyfriends and husbands). As performers, we get the best seat in the house. We notice pretty much everything that goes on during the course of the evening but whatever observation we make, it's none of our business. We must keep it to ourselves.

Remember: your job is to entertain the customers. That's it.

Speaking of personal lives, keep yours private from the customers as well. Drunk people like to talk. You may have only told one person that you and your girlfriend broke up last weekend, but by the time you perform on that stage again, the rest of the audience will know too. Let people hear your music, and keep your drama for your mama.

You also need to keep your band members' lives private. If some girl asks if your singer is single, you can politely remove yourself by saying, "I have no idea." Don't answer personal questions on behalf of other musicians. You may think it's harmless to answer, but it could end up causing a lot of problems. The same applies if one audience member asks you about someone else in the crowd. Don't answer personal questions on their behalf.

Remember the three monkeys: hear no evil, see no evil, speak no evil. Following that example will save your asses.

Find the Big Spenders

No matter what business you run, it's important to take care of the big spenders, and gigging in bars is no different.

Show everyone love on the floor, but if one guy is spending four dollars and another is spending a grand, the big spender should get a bit more attention from a business perspective.

Check out what people are sipping on. If one guy is nursing a Heineken all night he's still as important a customer; maybe he's not a big drinker or he has to drive. Nevertheless, if table eight is on their second bottle of Johnnie Walker Blue, they are most likely considered VIP by the establishment because they are dropping some serious dough. Always treat everyone with respect, but don't be naive: big spenders get more attention in any business.

Finally, keep an eye on sales. The bar owner is running a business and he needs to make money, so show him you're keeping an eye on how it's going each night. Bar owners have told me, "You know, Georges, you're the only musician who ever asks about the sales. I really appreciate that, man."

When my band started gigging, I wanted to break the sales records everywhere we played—I still do. It's fun to give ourselves a challenge, but it also proves to the bar owner that we're in this together, that the success of his bar is important to us, and that we are a band worth hiring and rehiring.

THE MUSICIAN'S NETWORK

Floor time is about developing a relationship with the audience and creating a community around the shared experience in the bar. Before you enter the crowd, remind yourself that these are not your customers, and then treat them right. If you do, they will come back and tell others, and your bar owner partners will love you for it. Respect the stage, but respect the floor too.

In the final section, the Encore, we'll gather all of the tips and tools that we've discussed so far and systematize them into something you can recreate again and again, even when shit happens.

CHALLENGE

SPREAD THE LOVE

The next time you do a gig, play a little game between sets. Divide the bar into sections—bar left, bar right, back tables, and so on—and send your bandmates into the crowd with these instructions: "Go out and say hello to people in your section. Collect the names of two guests—not ten, just two—and then jot them down backstage. Later on you can write down everything that you remember from your brief conversation with them: spouse's name, kids' names, dog's name, favorite song, favorite drink, and so on. Then share the names and info with your bandmates."

After the next set, have musicians go back out and take turns introducing other members of the band to the two people that they met earlier. Hang out, have some fun, then when you go back onstage, give a few shout-outs to some of the people that you met.

After the third set, go back out and introduce your two people to another two people in the audience you now know because your bandmate introduced you to them during the last break. Have everyone in the band do the same.

When you get back onstage, take a good look at what magic you've created! Listen to the buzz of friendship and laughter. People who walked in the club as strangers are now sharing stories like long-time friends. And you did that! You made a whole room of people happy. You just changed the world!

When many of those guests are wondering where to go the following weekend, where do you think they're going to go? People get addicted to that kind of joyful atmosphere.

Write a short story of how you packed the club, share it on social media, and tag me with #floor-time #gigforlife.

ENCORE

SYSTEMATIZE IT

Around 2000, I had to travel from Surabaya, Indonesia, to Hong Kong for a gig, which meant I had to pack, and packing stressed me out. My anxiety started building three or four weeks before I had to fly, mainly because I had to pack a lot of shit. It wasn't just clothes and shoes; I had to pack my drum throne, cymbals, sticks, snare, high hat, desktop computer, and music equipment the size of a fridge. It was like traveling with a whole studio.

After the gig ended three months later, I had to pack all over again for my trip to Canada, and my anxiety returned. I was disgusted by the whole process. As I sat there staring at the open suitcases and road cases, I had an idea. I took a roll of duct tape and slapped a piece to each case and numbered them one, two, three, and so on. Then I took out my laptop, opened a blank spreadsheet, and typed in Bag One, Bag Two, Bag Three.

As I picked up each item and put it in one of the suitcases, I wrote the name of the item in the spreadsheet. Under Bag One, for example, I put "day clothes" and then listed the day clothes that I was packing: three black T-shirts, running shoes, and so on. Under Bag Two I wrote "show clothes" and listed what I put in. I followed the same procedure for the computer, drum pieces, and music equipment. The whole time, I remained calm. In no time, I was done.

I had felt so stressed for years over a problem that I solved in about two hours.

That was twenty-three years ago, and I still use the same packing sheet when I travel. Over time I have modified this spreadsheet to better suit my needs and to cover other types of trips, such as "Three-Day Vacation" and "Cold Weather Country," and I have started packing in blocks or stacks (a stack for workout clothes, a stack for T-shirts and pajamas, a stack for dress slacks, and so on), but the system has basically stayed the same. It's always better to have something written down and then tweak it, rather than have nothing. As a friend of mine says, version one is better than version none. I also realized that with everything written down, I could hand this process off to someone else if need be and they could pack without my input—big bonus because I still hate packing.

This simple process relieved so much stress that I soon asked myself, *What else can I systematize?* Turns out, a lot.

If you think about your life, you'll realize that about 80 percent of everything you do is repetitive, things you do on a daily, weekly, monthly, or yearly basis, and 20 percent is new and creative. By systematizing the repetitive tasks, you can save your time and energy for the creative.

My rule of thumb is to systematize anything you know you're going to do more than once, whether professional or personal: contacting potential musicians and clubs, keeping track of contacts, rehearsals, remembering dance moves at different points in a song, cleaning the refrigerator, paying bills, buying a gift for your wife's birthday—everything.

This track will break down ways to systematize your life.

A CAUTIONARY TALE

My best friend and business partner, Marc, is a Canadian citizen who had been living in Taiwan for nearly ten years and was close to receiving permanent resident status. To remain in the country legally, however, he had to renew his residency every year.

One year Marc missed the deadline by one day—just one day—and as a result, the Taiwanese government deleted all of his previous years of residency, as if he never lived there. He had to leave everything behind, fly to Canada, and spend two months getting his papers in order. When he returned to Taiwan, he had to start all over as a brand new resident.

A year after that disaster, Marc called me and said, "Georges, you'll be proud of me."

"Oh yeah? What did you do?" I asked.

"I renewed my residency today, and I wrote everything down. I had a sample of the form, I had the exact address, I had everything."

My bro learned the hard way how important it is to systematize. If he had simply put it in the calendar, with a reminder two months before, along with the address of the agency, an empty form, and a filled-out form for reference, it would have been just a routine process. He would have saved himself a lot of stress and headache. But because he didn't systematize, he had ten years of residency deleted just like that because he was one day late.

WHAT TO SYSTEMATIZE

To discover what you should systematize, do a little exercise: make a list of *everything* you do on a daily, weekly, monthly, and yearly basis: put gas in the car, renew your driver's license, mow the lawn, pay the electric bill, go to rehearsal, vacation. Write down everything you can think of.

Then sit back and ask yourself three questions:

- What can I automate?
- What can I delegate?
- What can I eliminate?

These questions come from Timothy Ferriss's book *The 4-Hour Workweek*, which has helped me systematize every area of my business and personal life, saving me tons of time and headache.

First, look at your list and figure out what you can *automate* once, so you don't have to think about it every week or month or however often it comes up. For instance, I used to worry about my bill payments back in Canada as I lived in other countries. Every month I'd have to sit down, find my bills, add them up, and send the required money back to Canada. One day I was fed up. I sat down and figured out all of my payments for the entire year and sent that lump sum to my bank account in Canada every January. I then set up automatic payments for all of my bills and credit cards. Done. Because it's automated, I only have to think about them once a year instead of every month.

Next, look at your list and ask yourself, "How much of what I have to do can be done by someone else? What can others do better or faster than me?" In other words, figure out what you can *delegate*.

After I identified everything that someone else could do, I hired an assistant to do it for me. Now, every Thursday my PA sends me a report of what she completed and what's coming up. Delegation took so many menial, yet still important, tasks off my plate. I think everyone should have a personal assistant, regardless of how much money you're making. Just check out Fiverr or Upwork, and you'll find someone who's looking for this kind of work.

The key to delegation is to batch tasks together into one function—paying all of the bills, doing all of the shopping, cleaning the whole house—and then delegate the function. Write up a spreadsheet that explains each function and what's involved, create tutorials to go along with each function, and add dates when each should be completed. Then hand off the spreadsheet. Done. If you change assistants, which happens to me every couple of years, just share the sheet with the next person. Ask for a weekly report of what was done the week before and what's coming up this week. Make comments in each cell if need be, and that is it. It takes ten minutes each week to read and respond to the report. If anything changes in the details the assistant updates it, and you're done forever.

Finally, look at the remaining items on your list and figure out what you can *eliminate*. Ask yourself, "Do I really want to do this anymore? Is it really necessary?" If not, then stop! You'd be amazed at how much you can clean up your life if you get rid of needless tasks. Often, it's the daily nags that bring us the most stress, not the large jobs. It's having to mow the lawn, to pay the electricity bills, even to pick up some milk. All these little things add up to create an enormous amount of repetitive stress that creates an endless loop of frustration.

On your list, you likely have tasks that only come up once a year (car registration), or every three to five years (driver's license), or every ten years (passport). If you're like me, you might forget exactly what you need to do when the time comes. The answer? Systematize it. Create a digital file and document the process for each task, even if it seems inconvenient at the time. Do it once, and do it in real time—as soon as you do the task the next time, document it while it's still fresh in your mind, and you'll never have to do it again.

Let's take your passport, for example. Next time you have to renew it, take a picture of the blank form and then the completed form. Add a page with a link to the website and notes about filling out any special fields that you don't want to forget. Set a reminder in your phone to get a photograph and to submit everything way ahead of the expiration date. Next time, the process will be much smoother. I've hired great musicians that couldn't come out on the road because their passports were invalid. It's a shame and something that's easily avoided.

Although systematizing doesn't require advanced software, if you can avoid relying on your brain, go ahead and do it. Use apps, photos, videos, spreadsheets, and digital notes—anything that helps you take care of the monotonous, repetitive things that you'd rather not do.

It is impossible to separate you, the person, from you, the musician. The more stressed you are in your personal life, the more stressed and less capable you'll be in your professional life, and vice versa. So we'll discuss how you can systematize both aspects, starting with your professional life.

Professional

Most of what you do as a musician is repetitive. Let's look at the most common functions you must perform on a regular basis and talk about how you can organize and systematize them to make your life easier.

REHEARSALS

We've said a lot about rehearsals, but the fact is, there's always a way to improve rehearsal. Always. You should continually look for ways to make rehearsals better, so that your shows can be better, so your floor time can be better, so you can keep getting the gigs you like and gain access to the ones that you really want.

Think about what goes on at each rehearsal. Which parts do you dread? Why? If you can't come up with the answer right away, walk yourself through each step: Learn your tune—is this the pain point? Drive to rehearsal—is this the pain point? The building itself; meeting with the band; the arguments over tune selection, endings, or harmonies; other people's lack of preparation—think through every single step to identify what you dread, and then figure out a way to systematize it so that it is no longer an issue. For example, if your pain point is the musician who is always unprepared, put a system in place to call him a couple of days before the rehearsal or assign another band member the job of doing a virtual rehearsal with the unprepared person. Sure, it's not your job to babysit, but better to be preemptive than to waste the whole band's time come rehearsal day. The other option, of course, is to replace the musician.

When I started to analyze rehearsals, I realized we didn't learn enough songs each year, so I asked myself, "What is the fastest, most efficient way to learn a tune? You break up a tune into parts." That's something I had done already using the forms I went over earlier in the book, but I took it a step further—I uploaded each tune that I wanted to learn into a software, and then using digital markers, I identified each part like this: verse one, verse two, chorus, bridge (see Figure 9.1). Now, I had a way to "see" the tune, had complete control over the tune, and knew which parts to go over.

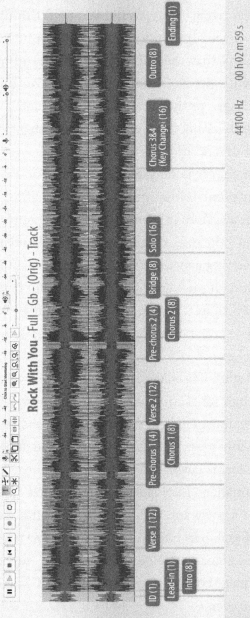

Rock With You - Full - Gb - (Orig) - Track

ID (1)
Lead-in (1)
Intro (8)
Verse 1 (12)
Pre-chorus 1 (4)
Chorus 1 (8)
Verse 2 (12)
Pre-chorus 2 (4)
Chorus 2 (8)
Bridge (8)
Solo (16)
Chorus 3&4 (Key Change) (16)
Outro (8)
Ending (1)

44100 Hz   00 h 02 m 59 s

Figure 9.1. Digital Markers in Software

Rock With You - Full - Gb - (Orig) - Track

ID (1) Lead-in (1) Intro (8) Verse 1 (12) Pre-chorus 1 (4) Chorus 1 (8)

44100 Hz 00 h 02 m 59 s

Although writing your forms on paper works just fine, the software shows sound waves for each section of the song; that wasn't something that I could easily recreate by hand. I realized that every verse is about thirty-two seconds, regardless of its tempo, because every song is about three and a half minutes long. From there, I realized that, in general, every song has two verses and five choruses, all with mostly the same lyrics. Then it dawned on me: *Why do we keep rehearsing the tune from beginning to end? There has to be a system to this.*

I put each song into the software, and then I pulled up the information on two screens (or on top of each other on the same screen if two screens were not available): on one, I had the original tune, and on the other, I had the lyrics. The lyrics were written in a way that reflected the music: paragraph one was verse one, paragraph two was verse two, and so on. It was so easy to see everything at once, so I could break things down into parts. If I knew my bass player had the chorus down, but he was foggy on the verses, I could cue the song in the software, right at the parts he needed to work on.

Software provides great advantages for practicing your songs. For example, let's say you are a singer and learning the lyrics for a new song, but you are struggling with the third sentence of the first verse. With the right software, you can loop that particular part of the song over and over again to isolate it instead of doing the whole verse. You can also slow it down a lot without changing the pitch. You can't really do this without software. It's cumbersome to try.

Software makes it easy. Once you load the tune, identify the sections, and name them, they are there forever. You can isolate sections, loop them, slow them down, speed them up—it's all at your fingertips.

Once I realized how well this system worked, I hired a full-time producer (shout out to Andrea Spolti) to do the tracks and forms for all of our bands using software, so we could learn and build our repertoire much faster.

REPERTOIRE

The goal is to gig for life, right? Which means that you're going to be doing a lot of shows. To make life easier, systematize the changes to your repertoire.

Here's a basic formula: If you average ten songs per set, you'll end up playing around forty songs per show. If you have three shows at the same club in the same week, you'll need a repertoire of 120 songs so that you can play a different show each night. That way if people come to see you twice during those three days, they won't see the same show twice. For each show, make sure that you have at least ten to fourteen A+ songs of the day, plus a few showstoppers that are sure to give people something to talk about.

A repertoire of 120 songs is really all you need. You only need to learn the classics like "Hotel California" once. In time, as you keep learning new songs, you'll have a surplus of material and the freedom to drop the duds and still maintain that collection of 120 songs. After you play the hot tunes for about four months, gradually drop them and then bring them back in a few years when they become the new classics.

Another reason for carefully building your repertoire is to keep your partners at the venues happy. If you're booked for a few months at a bar, management and the staff will hear the same songs repeatedly, and some of them may complain about your lack of creativity. Do what you can to mix it up, but there's not much you can do if they work there every night and hear the same tunes, so don't sweat it too much.

As mentioned in Track 6, we developed a system for ranking songs as A+, A, B, or C and then created sets in the shape of a W. Systematizing set creation drastically cut down on the time and stress we spent on this task at rehearsals.

We also systematized our wardrobe repertoire for the stage using the color palettes mentioned earlier. We have seven different palettes, so if we play six nights a week, we're not repeating the same palette twice. Plus, if someone comes to see the band every Monday, they're not seeing the same palette they saw the previous week.

To make it even easier on the bands, I created a graphic that lists all of the interchangeable color palettes, so they could see all of the possible colors they could wear and maximize outfit combinations for the sake of variety. For example, we have a fall palette, and the photos show light orange, brown, and green. We also have the piano, black and white; green and blue; and pastel. We always include all black, because it looks sharp and classy, and everyone has black in their wardrobe.

Remember: you still need to look like you're part of the show. You should stand out when you walk into Costco. But once you have those stylish clothes in the various palettes, you don't have to keep buying clothes. Systematizing the band's wardrobe like this really cuts down on uncertainty, cost, and time, but you still have freedom to be creative by mixing and matching and by accessorizing to change things up.

SETUP AND TEARDOWN

Setting up for a gig always takes longer than tearing down at the end of the night, so the setup in particular should be systematized. Drum sets have many pieces—stands, toms, pedals, cymbals, the seat, the sticks, microphones, wires, as well as a rug so that the drum set doesn't slide all over the place. After a gig, I'd usually enjoy some floor time and a couple of drinks, so by the time I was ready to dismantle the set, pack it, and head home, it was four in the morning, minus twenty degrees outside, and I was exhausted. Even though we were playing at the same club for the next two nights, I couldn't leave the drum set there because I had nothing else to practice on during the day to continue to fine-tune and learn the material.

Finally, I thought to myself, *Man, this sucks big time.* Solution: buy myself a second identical drum set, one for my studio and one for gigs, with the money I had already saved. That way, I could leave one set at the venue for the duration of the gig. This saved me so much time and stress.

Because a drum set is so important to a gig, you can't afford to have anything go wrong. If you lose or break a part, the show can come to a complete halt. So I made sure that I always had backup pieces like a pedal, kick drum head, and snare head. No matter what instrument you play, have backup parts as part of your system.

One day, I took my systematization even further: I customized my setup so that at every gig and regardless of the shape of the stage, I didn't have to think about where to put each piece. I took a roll of electrical tape and marked the rug where each piece of my drum set should go—my seat, snare stand, kick drum legs, cymbal stand legs, and so on. From then on, all I had to do was to match the shapes of the set with the shapes of tape on the rug. I also locked all of my cymbals and microphone stands at their respective height, so that I didn't need to adjust them every time. Setting up used to take a good forty minutes, but now it took a fraction of the time. Boom. Done.

BUY THE BEST

Here's a quick tip: when you buy music equipment, always buy the best. Don't buy shitty equipment in an effort to save money, because it'll probably break down or you'll be unsatisfied and you'll have to buy it all over again. Besides, crappy equipment sounds crappy. You are investing in your career. Even if that means saving money and waiting a while longer, it's worth it. Just start with the best.

GOING ONSTAGE

To respect the stage and to put on your best performance night after night, you need to be in a particular frame of mind—calm and focused. If you're running around trying to find your shirt or finish your makeup, you'll feel flustered and frustrated. You need a system for getting ready for each show so that you're in the zone the minute you walk onstage.

For me, that system looked like this: An hour before leaving for the show, I would kiss my son goodnight. My wife would draw me a bath, dim the lights, or even light a candle, and as I soaked, I would think about how I was going to walk onstage, what surprise I would have for the band and audience to get them all excited, and so on.

Because I had a system for wardrobe, my outfit would already be ready for me to put on, so no last-minute decisions to stress me out.

If you put it all in place ahead of time, you can devote all of your energy to delivering a Saturday night performance every night of the week.

TRAVEL

Life is enriched by the places you travel to and by the people you meet on the road, but as I've mentioned, getting from place to place can be incredibly stressful, and so can finding your way around once you get there.

Where do you want to go? Bangkok? Bali? Dubai? Montreal? Beijing? Seoul? Beirut? In any of those places, I can tell you where the airport lounge is, which restaurants serve the best breakfast, where you can have a shisha at night, and where to go for coffee. How can I provide this information in a matter of seconds? Because I've systematized my traveling process as well. I'm a local as soon as I arrive.

To travel efficiently, you need two things: assistance and organization. As mentioned, you can use Upwork or Fiverr to find an affordable assistant. Paying more cash for less stress is worth it to me. Even if you choose not to have an assistant, you can make great use of your smartphone. To organize places and people, you can use Google Sheets or apps like Apple Notes or Google Keep. I prefer

Apple Notes because I'm a very biased Apple nut. To me, Apple Notes is the best app on the iPhone, but with a variety of available apps, you can easily get the same result, so just pick your favorite.

The key to documenting and organizing your information is to put one item per note, rather than a list of items in one note. If you use one note for all of the places you visited in Beijing, for example, you'll have to scroll up and down to find the item you're looking for. However, if you use one item per note, when you search for Beijing you will get the results in a list view, making the one you want much easier to find. You could title the note with the name of the place and then add information and hashtags:

- The Rug Restaurant, Beijing (title)
- Great breakfast, great atmosphere, went there with Richard (information)
- #beijing, #breakfast (hashtags)

You can also add the map link and a picture from the last time you were there; I always do.

Now, next time you're in Beijing, take out your phone, search "Beijing" and "breakfast," and voilà! There is the place you are looking for, plus a few other favorites you've visited, documented forever.

It really only takes two minutes to jot down a new entry in your notes. Do that for all the places you go to, from train stations to restaurants, favorite taxi drivers, where to buy sim cards, and so on. The next time you go to that city again, you'll be roaming like a local.

With my system in place, I can also delegate some important tasks to my personal assistant, so she can coordinate with our logistics team for flights and ground transportation and book my meetings with management, band leaders, and individual musicians. There is a lot to do, so systematizing the process is essential.

I travel a lot, over two hundred days a year for many, many years now, so at this point in my life, I am blessed to have wonderful friends and acquaintances all over the world—Southeast Asia, the Middle East, Africa, China, Europe, South America, North America, you name it. Because there are so many, I have people categorized in a project management system and in my phone. Before I travel anywhere, my PA takes a look at all the cities I'll be visiting and creates a list of all of the people that I'll want to see during my stay. Either she or I will contact them ahead of time, to let them know that I'll be in town between this date and that date so that we can plan important meetings or simply to catch up for dinner and drinks. Over the years, this system has helped me maintain these wonderful relationships across the globe.

I've been robbed while traveling, so now I carry two wallets with me everywhere I go. Both have cash and credit cards. I keep one on me and one in my carry-on, which is also packed according to another system. My laptop and iPad each have their own sleeve, and I place all of the wires, plugs, and chargers in a special wire pad. Documentation such as my passport goes in one of the inside pockets. I put each item in its designated place every time. This way I always know exactly where everything is. I also have a system for packing and unpacking my suitcases when I'm on the road. I don't use drawers or closets at the hotel (unless I need to hang a suit). I simply take out the six to eight stacks of clothes from my suitcase and place them on the couch or on top of the dresser. Even if I'm only staying for one night, I completely empty my suitcase because I end up having to unpack everything in order to repack, even if I only use a few items. Better to take everything out in neat stacks right away and then replace the neat stacks when it's time to leave. Quick and easy.

When it's time for me to leave the hotel, I put the clean stacks back in the suitcase, cover them all with an unfolded T-shirt, and place the dirty clothes on top so that they're immediately accessible when I want to send them to laundry services at the next hotel. By not using storage in hotel rooms, I save time because all of my clothes, clean and used, are right where I can see them. This also minimizes the risk of leaving items behind, and my last-minute room check takes less than a minute.

COMPUTERS

Have you ever lost or broken your laptop or had it stolen? Did you happen to have a half-written term paper on it that you hadn't saved to an external hard drive? It's the kind of shit that gives you nightmares long into adulthood.

All of the above circumstances have happened to me in the past, but if they happened now, I wouldn't lose one thing. You could destroy any of my devices and I wouldn't care, other than from a monetary perspective. I mean, it would be a hassle to replace everything, but I wouldn't mourn any lost files, because I never store anything on my computer or any other device, ever.

My team is all over the globe, and we all need access to the same documents, so it doesn't make sense to have people store them on their computers. Instead, we store everything in the cloud using Google Workspace, where everyone has access to all the information that we share, 24/7. We've been using Google apps since 2007, before the cloud was even a thing.

I highly recommend that you work in a shared cloud environment. Google is probably the easiest since most people have a Gmail account or can easily create one. With Google, you have the whole suite of products at your disposal: Google Drive, Meet, Chat, Docs, Sheets, Calendar, and more.

Software, alone, is an amazing way to systematize your life.

BLOGS

If you write blog posts for your business, or even a personal blog, do yourself a favor and systematize it. For a while, the same thing would happen every year in my company. One of my staff members would say, "Hey, Halloween is in two weeks. What are we going to write about?" Or "Christmas is coming up. What are we going to do?"

Christmas is not something new. It's been coming at that date for more than two thousand years, and it's going to come up every year going forward. Why not sit down in January and write your blog posts and banners for Christmas, New Year's, Halloween, Thanksgiving, and every other holiday way ahead of time? In fact, have one brainstorming session to write out fifty-two posts, one for each week of the year. Send them to your graphic designer to put in captions and photos, keep them in a folder, and schedule release them once a week. You can even schedule their weekly release all at the same time, so you don't waste time on that either.

KIT PROFILES

In 1988, I read Harvey Mackay's book *Swim with the Sharks Without Being Eaten Alive* and learned the importance of learning about people you meet and keeping track of that information. Soon after, I created a system for keeping track of everyone I meet. I call them KITs, my "Keep in Touch" profiles.

In my KITs, I keep track of all kinds of information that I learn about each person from our conversations—name, significant other, birthdates, kids' names and ages—and I update the file whenever I talk to the person if I have anything significant to add. I also have reminders to contact people on a regular basis. If Sam gave me a gig all the way back in 1987, I'll still call him once a year. After we talk, I immediately record myself dictating any new information that I'd like to update for future reference, such as: "Had a great chat with Sam. He has a new baby named Jude. His mom recently passed away."

Here again, having a personal assistant comes in handy. She and I have a system where I record thoughts after meetings and personal conversations and put them in a shared note. The next morning when she starts her day, she checks for new notes, then processes and deletes them. I even use video when I'm recording so that she can see my mouth, emotions, and body language. This makes it easier for her to transcribe, interpret my tone on various topics, and not misunderstand certain words in case the audio is unclear. It makes for better communication all around.

I organize my KIT profiles into different categories:

- A+: mom, siblings, nephews and nieces, best friend, key business contacts
- A: good friends, distant relatives

- B: club owners, colleagues, bandmates, and other acquaintances
- C: people I've met but have no ongoing relationship with

Then I decide how often I want to contact each group. For me, the A+ people are contacted weekly or every other week, the As are monthly, and the Bs are every three to six months. The Cs are probably people that I contact once a year on their birthday, during various religious holidays, or to send a Happy New Year's text or video. I enter dates in my calendar, and I set reminders as backup.

No matter who it is, you might be tempted to say "Happy Birthday!" on their Facebook page. I recommend sending a direct message or, better yet, send a short video greeting, less than a minute. People love to see your face and hear your voice.

I also use KIT profiles to help me remember birthdays, anniversaries, and other important dates. To keep track of people's ages, I use a code with my age as a point of reference. For example, "G -2" means the person is two years younger than me. For people's kids, I write something like "J +3," so I know the person's son or daughter is three years older than my son Julian. I will not forget my age or my son's age, and I don't have time to figure out what age someone is if they were born in 1986.

I consider myself to be a caring person, but I know that I can be forgetful and suffer from information overload sometimes, so I let the system do the work. I assign one day a week to writing messages, and then I spend an hour connecting with people. Having a system is a lifesaver!

Personal

You might be surprised by how many aspects of your personal life can be systematized, everything from hobbies to charities to preparing for your death. (Sorry to be morbid, but death is inevitable—although I'm in no hurry.)

MICROSYSTEMS

A close cousin to systematizing is the checklist. I'm a checklist nut; I have them for everything from trips to the grocery store to hobbies like golf. Checklists are a key part of microsystems, which capture all the smaller tasks within the bigger tasks you want and need to complete.

Let's take golf, for example. I'm three levels below terrible at this game, but I still play because it's a great way to connect with my friends and to meet people. So I made a checklist of everything that I need to do pre-game, so that all of my spare time is actually spent having fun with my buddies, not getting ready for the fun. Thanks to the checklist, anytime a friend calls to ask if I'm free for a game, I'm ready to go: clubs, balls, tees, and, of course, a couple of good cigars.

Within checklists, I use micro-tutorials for the tasks that are complicated or have a lot of steps. In these micro-tutorials I include videos, photos of empty and filled-out forms, detailed instructions—whatever is needed to help someone complete the task. Let's stick with the passport example. I have a preset reminder in my calendar, and inside the calendar event, there's a link to the checklist of tasks to complete. My assistant uses the micro-tutorials within the tasks to help her carry out the steps. In one of the videos, I recorded myself clicking through the website to get to the correct forms, which she prepares. Then I just need to get my mug shot and head to the consulate. When I get there, I check my notes, where I've included details such as "the agent's office, fourth floor." This fool-proof system turns a nuisance of a task into a more pleasant experience.

When I create checklists and micro-tutorials, I imagine I'm talking to someone who has never done the task before. I ask myself and my team, "If you were not here tomorrow, would another person be able to do this task flawlessly without asking a single question?" Then I make sure that all steps to achieving any task are detailed and documented through micro-tutorials. The next time someone has to repeat the task, they simply follow the steps, and they can execute it seamlessly.

Now say that I need to hire a driver to take me to the airport or to drive my family to the beach. I pull up my checklist, and I can see that Raul is the guy I want to book because he's qualified, and I remember enjoying the ride. If he's unavailable, I'll ask for the next best driver that

I've hired in the past. I also include a list of which drivers to never ask for again and why. It's all there in my notes, including their photos. That way I can also have someone else book the right driver for me.

Now that I have people helping me book gigs and drive bands around all over the world, we update our providers/suppliers list after every weekly team meeting. Someone may say that one driver has moved or that they found another gopher to help with transportation of stuff. Someone else might share that they had a bad experience with another driver. We remove the names that we're no longer using and add the new ones along with a photo and contact info. We do this with every aspect of our business, not just drivers.

Have you ever walked into the kitchen for your morning coffee, only to find out that you're out of milk? Or you walk into your office and your favorite pen is gone or your chair is out of place or no one added paper in the printer? These are first-world problems, I know, but they can still irritate the shit out of you. So create microsystems to make sure that your things and affairs are always in order.

The same actions are required for a simple grocery list for home and for your office. Divide those lists into items that need to be bought weekly or monthly. Take photos of how you want the refrigerator shelves, kitchen cabinets, and drawers organized; do the same for your office. Now it's clear where things should go once they are bought.

When we first moved to Vietnam, we lived and performed in a beautiful five-star hotel. At the lobby level, they had many high-end retail stores, including Gucci. The store manager was friends with my wife, so we would wait inside near the front of the store for our six-year-old son, Julian, to return from school. He would run from the bus straight into the store and start playing hide-and-seek. He would slide under tables and wiggle under displays. The staff knew exactly where he was, and they'd giggle while looking in his direction.

After watching this happen several times, the manager gave Julian her iPad with pictures of all the displays and said, "Go find every item on the shelves and match them with each photo." Excited, he walked from section to section, adjusting all the clothes that didn't belong on one shelf and put them on the right shelf. He arranged all of the shoes so they matched the photos. He could do this because Gucci had their shit together. They had systematized the layout and all of the displays, so the store would look exactly as intended every single day. This is the power of having a system. Theirs was so perfect and simple that even a child could do it.

If any of your projects involve three or more people, I recommend using project management software such as Wrike, ClickUp, or Monday.com. A band fits into this category since you are regularly scheduling rehearsals, extra dance practice, gigs, and so on. Software like this is even more important if you're trying to put two or three bands together or if you are collaborating with other bands. By now you understand that all tasks, big and small, demand organization—otherwise things can quickly become complex. You don't want to be drafting endless and confusing emails or to lose track of something important in the WhatsApp feed.

The best types of systems are project- and task-oriented. This way you can break everything down, communicate clearly about specific tasks, and know exactly which ones have been completed. And when you start a similar project, you can simply upload the template and assign people their responsibilities.

One of my favorite things about these platforms is that they eliminate the need for a lot of nonsensical, unnecessary meetings. For example, instead of having to arrange a meeting between several people, I simply assign someone a task at my leisure. Then at their leisure, they can work on it and ask for feedback. Every task has an owner and a deadline, clearly laid out so the task can be shared and others can be tagged to be brought in the loop. No need for an official, whole meeting to take place.

The system works even better if you communicate back and forth via video recordings. I can record myself telling someone to learn a tune, assign the task, attach the tune, and send it off. If they have a question they follow up as needed. Later, I can open up my software and see what tasks have or haven't been done. I run my entire business like this, no matter where I am in the world. Not a *thing* happens in my company that I don't know about.

CHARITY

When I was three years old, I had an operation that changed my life. I was born with a cleft palate, and the surgery helped people see me for who I was, not the flaws on my face. If that hadn't happened, I wouldn't be the person I am today. My band was called Scarlip for a reason: what used to make me super shy became my badge of honor.

Now my thing is helping other children with a cleft palate benefit from the same surgery. I joined Smile Train and began helping one child a year. However, some years I would forget, and I would feel horrible. So I systematized it. I started donating money on my birthday and six months later. As my own financial situation has improved over time, I set up an automated monthly payment to be able to do six kids' lips every year. My plan is to eventually help one child every month and maybe one day, help one kid every week.

If you choose to make an impact on society, think about which causes are truly meaningful to you, and systematize your gifts. You'll be changing lives for the better without wasting good brain space trying to remember when to donate.

DOCUMENTS AND INFORMATION

In Track 10, we'll talk about creating a What If list that includes your death, but here let's talk about how to systematize important documents and information to make life easier for you and your family. You can organize your documents in a filing cabinet, upload them digitally to your Google Drive, organize the information in an Excel sheet—whatever works best for you. I love working with digital mind maps with clickable links to all the important files and documents.

For example, in one branch of my mind map I have Banking, where I list the names of banks, accounts, and countries (we've lived in many countries!). Should anything happen to me, my wife and son can easily access all of these accounts.

Another branch of my mind map reads Important Documents. That's where I list my most important documents such as birth certificates, marriage certificate, high school and university diplomas, driver's license, health cards, passports, car insurance, house ownership documents, homeowner's insurance, final will, investments, credit cards, and so on. I list each document as a separate note, and I include a photo or a couple of seconds' video shot with my iPhone showing where the hard copies are located, whether it's a drawer, safety deposit box, or whatever. I also include a photo of the item itself, for example, front and back of each credit card. Last year my brother-in-law was staying at our house in Canada. He called me in Vietnam to ask if I had an extra car key. I sent him a ten-second video titled "Extra Car Key" that I had saved in my Apple Notes. My brother-in-law found the key in thirty seconds. He still tells the story. I also make these videos for myself, because I always forget where things are since I'm generally only in Canada once a year.

I also have a complete investment philosophy and how-to video tutorial for my son, in which I explain my strategies: how and why I invest; the ratio of the portfolio; the minimum and maximum number of companies I should hold at any given time; how long I will hold the company, no matter what happens on a daily or quarterly basis; when I should rebalance my portfolio; and at what ratio I should hold every position. I've color-coded everything to make it as easy as possible for Julian to follow.

Every year I update the information in my When I'm Gone system, accompanied with a short video of me explaining what I'm doing. I use OBS software to record the clicks I'm making on the screen as I talk, and I share the video with two or three people, so they remember this system exists and know where all the stuff is if anything happens to me. You're not just systematizing the documents and information for yourself but for your family and friends too. Some of you may have gone through a nightmarish inheritance story. It usually happens because the deceased didn't think through what would happen after they died. The result is enormous stress that can tear families apart for decades. This can be avoided if you create a system now.

BREAKS

If you don't plan to take time off, you will burn out. So why not plan ahead and systematize it? Long vacations stress me out, so I prefer to plan regular shorter getaways. Pick a system that works for you, whether it's one weekend a month or three weeks every January.

Another benefit of systematizing your breaks is that you always have something to look forward to, and anticipation is good for the soul. Be as serious about your vacations as you are about your work.

READING

I love to read because I love to learn. Though I read a lot, I'm not very good at retaining information. As soon as I start a new book, many of the lessons from the previous book are gone. I finally got sick of this happening, so I systematized reading too.

I used to use a mind map to summarize each chapter, but now I simply share what I'm learning with anyone who will listen. Talking to others about what I've learned helps me absorb the lessons so they become part of me. If I can't explain it and teach it, I don't know it. This drives my friends nuts. "Oh, you want to learn about investing? Let me show you how to get started. I read a book about that recently..." I try to integrate what I learned right away, so it becomes a part of my daily routine.

If you're like me, there's too much going on in your brain to remember all that you've read. Come up with a way to keep track of what you learn so that you can use it.

READING LIST

Here's a list of the books mentioned in this track and in Track 10. I've found them helpful in systematizing my life and in working on my financial picture:

- *Can't Hurt Me* by David Goggins
- *The Checklist Manifesto* by Atul Gawande
- *Getting Things Done* by David Allen
- *The Effective Executive* by Peter F. Drucker
- *The E-Myth Revisited* by Michael E. Gerber
- *The 4-Hour Workweek* by Timothy Ferriss
- *How to Win Friends and Influence People* by Dale Carnegie
- *One Up on Wall Street* by Peter Lynch
- *Rich Dad Poor Dad* by Robert T. Kiyosaki
- *Rule #1* by Phil Town
- *The 7 Habits of Highly Effective People* by Stephen Covey

- *Swim with the Sharks Without Being Eaten Alive*
  by Harvey Mackay

EMOTIONS

In life, disagreements are inevitable, but they don't have to linger and lead to resentment and unhappiness. You can develop a system for resolving the conflict when it happens and avoid the long-term consequences. Yes, the heated conversation might make you very uncomfortable. Still, it's better to rip the Band-Aid off than live with festering anger and unhappiness.

So how do you systematize happiness in this area? When you find yourself in conflict with someone, stop and try to pinpoint what the core of the argument is about, and write it down. If you do this consistently, you may notice that you usually argue about the same things with the same people. This is when you take a moment to sit down with them and say, "You know, it seems like we're always arguing about this. What do you say we try to find a solution, so that way we can fix this together once and for all?"

Because you're aware of what you tend to argue about, you can change your action or reaction the next time the situation arises and perhaps avoid the argument altogether. Perhaps you can also change your own actions that may be contributing to the conflict. Whatever you do, don't walk around with resentment. If a disagreement still arises, you can talk about it right then and there, clear the air, and resume harmony. In the end, the idea is to pre-empt arguments and discord in order to have great relationships and minimize stress.

As we'll talk about in more detail in Track 10, shit happens in life. Your refrigerator breaks down, you lose your phone, you get into a car accident. These situations can really affect our mood and make us feel angry, bitter, frustrated, even depressed at times. But you can systematize those emotions as well, by thinking through what might happen in life, so you are not shocked when it does.

One night when I was about nineteen, my friends and I went to a club. As soon as I parked the car, the entire muffler dropped to the ground. I was a kid, and that was probably going to cost me a lot of money. Still, after we got out of the car and realized what happened, I turned toward my friends and said, "Okay, let's go."

"What?" one of my friends asked. "Aren't you angry?"

"No, we're here to have fun. Let's go."

"But why aren't you angry?"

"I always knew that the car would break down one day. I just didn't know when. Why get mad? I knew it would happen someday. And that someday is now. I can't do anything about it tonight, so I'll deal with it tomorrow. In the meantime, let's go have some fun."

Without having a name for it, I had already been systematizing my emotions, specifically frustration and anger, by being prepared for shit to hit the fan. Full disclosure: emotions still get the best of me. I've been hot-blooded my whole life, but those who know me vouch that it's a fraction of how I used to be. This system helped me immensely.

HOW TO SYSTEMATIZE

Now you know what to systematize; how do you go about doing it? The most important thing to remember is, *document everything.*

On my computer, I have folders and subfolders to document both personal and professional systems that I've created. I have folders for wardrobe, set lists, lyrics, forms, KIT profiles, reading lists—everything. Inside those folders are subfolders with checklists, photos, videos, and searchable notes related to the system.

For example, I love trying new food and new restaurants, so I have notes about which restaurants I like for breakfast or for dinner and in which city and country, along with map links, photos of my favorite plates, and who I went with. In the Home Cleaning folder, my assistant Annie has notes for the refrigerator. She took pictures of how the inside should be organized—where the drinks should go, the eggs, and so on. She created a timeline and calendar reminder that goes off when it's time to clean the fridge, weekly and monthly shopping lists for the home and office, the allocated budget, and exactly where to find the stuff. Annie just graduated and moved on to conquer the world. All she had to do was hand over G's Assistant Manual to the next person. I had a thirty-minute handover meeting with the new person, and that was it. No need to train her. It's all there, systematized.

I know. It seems like a lot of information to retain. Remember, I've created these systems over a period of forty years. The important thing is to start. The next time you have a delicious breakfast out, take a photo of the menu, write a note like "Great American Breakfast," and add a few tags (#breakfast, #restaurant, #Montreal). Now you have your first entry in your Dining folder. Bon appetit!

To make your system user friendly, you have to name, label, and tag in an intelligent way so that you will always remember where to find what you need. Whenever you create a new folder or add hashtags to a note, ask yourself, "How will I find this six months from now? How will someone else find this six months from now?" Decide now whether you will use #pic, #picture, #pix, #photo, or #photograph, and stick to one so you don't drive yourself crazy trying to remember every time you search for something. Naming and tags are much more important than folders and subfolders. Even if you don't want to create folders or forget to, if you name and tag properly, you will find what you are looking for.

Another tip: always take photos and videos to include with each note, whether it's to document a process or the person who went with you to that great restaurant that you both loved or simple instructions on how to find the small parking lot down the street from the bar. Smartphones make this so easy.

I read a great tip from Jeff Bezos: take one picture a day. It works almost like your journal. Once you see the picture, you'll remember the highlights of that day. Apple and Google photo apps can search objects and animals, like "duck" or "bicycle." The other day I broke my own rule on documenting and couldn't find an address, so I just searched Google Photos for Restaurant, Fish, Dominican Republic, and the picture came right up. I clicked on the photo details, and it gave me all the info, including the exact address of where that photo was taken. Technology used properly can be very helpful and fun.

To get the most out of your systems, you also need to add a "control mechanism" to make sure you're still using the system a month or a year from now and that it's still decreasing stress and saving you time. The control mechanism could be a checklist, report, reminder, annual review, survey, or inspection. The goal is simply to check in with yourself or your team to find out if the systems are working and keep on working when you move on to other priorities.

Feedback is another effective control mechanism. With Uber, every customer rates their driver. If the customer gives a bad review, Uber can address the issue immediately. They have a system and a control mechanism in place that tells them when certain aspects of their business are falling apart without having to constantly watch every driver.

Systematization is an ongoing, never-ending process of making your life easier.

GIVE YOURSELF A BREAK

Your life is a moving, grooving, repetitive machine. It's all too easy to drop the ball when you're trying to juggle so many at once. Give yourself a break and systematize anything that doesn't need your direct, immediate intervention. Remove yourself from the "bottleneck," and let the system carry the stress. That repetitive stuff simply isn't worth the mindspace required to keep track of it all. All that overthinking can weigh you down.

Stop doing the things you don't want to do. Create, customize, and implement the best systems to take care of those things. The more you put on autopilot, the more mental and emotional space you free up to enjoy life, family, and friends. You'll also be better prepared to deal with the big life problems that may come your way.

USE YOUR PHONE

Go buy plastic sleeves from an office supply store and block out two hours in your schedule. Then grab a coffee or your favorite beverage, find a comfortable space, and empty your wallet, your purse, your file cabinet, wherever you've stored your credit cards and your life documents—passport, insurance, car registration, birth certificate, and so on. Lay them all out on the floor or on your desk. One pizza at a time, we're going to create a system.

Grab the document on top and take a picture of it. Share it to notes, title it, and tag it (e.g., Passport—Rachel, #importantdocuments). Once you're done documenting digitally, take the physical document and slip it in a plastic sleeve. If it's a single-page document like a birth certificate, you put it in one sleeve. If it's the registration of your house and it's many pages long, put all ten in the same sleeve. Once done, place the sleeves in a filing cabinet or drawer or wherever you feel comfortable, and put your credit cards back in your wallet or purse.

Now, take your phone again and videotape yourself while you record the locations. "Hello future me or someone I love, this is where you'll find the passports, and here is where you'll find the birth certificates," and so on. Share this to your note and title it and tag it (Important Documents—physical location, #importantdocuments #physical #location #stored). Use whatever naming system works for you, so the future you or someone else that you shared the notes with can find them intuitively.

Write a post of how you feel about cleansing and taking things out of your head and placing them somewhere to process, share on social media, and tag me with #systematize #gigforlife.

SHIT HAPPENS

"Georges, what happened at the bar where you were playing last night?" my friend asked when I answered the phone.

"What do you mean, what happened?"

"It's gone."

"What do you mean it's gone?"

"It's gone. Someone bombed it. There's nothing left."

I drove to the bar and found all of my equipment in the wreckage—my drum set, mics, my sampler, Mike's guitar amp. Everything was melted or completely blown to shit. I had borrowed money from my brother Nick to buy that sampler, and I still owed him for it.

Around the same time I was working my side business doing sound engineering for all of the major Arabic stars who came from overseas to perform in Ottawa and Montreal. The owner of a Lebanese restaurant had asked me to install a permanent sound system in his restaurant. "Don't worry, Georges, I'll pay you later," he assured me. Since it was quite expensive as a lump sum, I let him pay installments of five hundred bucks a month.

About four months after I installed the system, I got a phone call from a Lebanese musician. "Georges, the restaurant is gone."

"What are you talking about?" I asked.

"It got hit by Lebanese lightning."

"What the fuck is Lebanese lightning?"

"It's when an owner can't make his payments anymore, so he sets his own restaurant on fire, so he can receive the insurance payment," my friend explained.

The insurance company paid the owner for *my* sound equipment, but the owner never sent me the money, and he somehow disappeared. Thousands of dollars up in flames.

As you well know by now, shit happens in life: a death in the family, a severe personal injury, war, a pandemic, money lost in the stock market, natural disasters, robberies, fires that torch equipment—you name it. Any number of things could really sink you when you're caught off guard and unprepared. In this track we'll discuss the importance of planning for life's unexpected emergencies. If you don't, they could bring on more than just stress; they could wipe out everything that you've built.

Full disclosure: I am not a financial advisor. I'm merely sharing what has worked for me and continues to do so. In addition to the suggestions shared here, I recommend reading some of the financial books mentioned in Track 9.

MAKE A "WHAT IF?" LIST

As mentioned in the last track, one way to systematize emotions is to think about bad things that could happen, and accept that they probably will, so that you're not shocked when they do. That was how I stayed unaffected when my muffler fell out. In comparison with other things that happen in life, car troubles are not that bad. I recommend making a "What If" list to help you prepare for the really big shit that can come your way, events that could wipe out you or your family financially. Ask yourself, *What if, what if, what if?* and write down every single thing that pops into your head, for example:

- What if I lose my job?
- What if a bar closes?
- What if someone in my family gets in a severe accident?
- What if I have to move on a moment's notice?
- What if I get sued?
- What if I get a divorce?
- What if I get cancer?
- What if I died tomorrow?

Then, ask yourself, In case that happens, what should I do now to prepare? For example:

- If I lose my job, I'll have to dip into my savings. I need to start saving 25 percent of my income immediately to save for another "rainy day."If a bar shuts down—or gets blown up in my case—I'll lose the future scheduled gigs at that venue. I need to maintain my KIT profiles and contact other bar owners, so I can book my band elsewhere as soon as possible.

- If someone in my family gets into an accident, I will take some time off of work to help them. This is another reason to continually save for a rainy day.

- If I have to move suddenly, I will use my savings or preferably my emergency fund. I need to create an emergency fund, separate from my savings. This is another reason to maintain my KIT file, so I can ask some close friends for a few strong arms.

- If I get sued, I can contact an attorney. I need to find a lawyer now. More importantly, I need to incorporate my band, so that if I get sued, the company may go down and not me.

- If I get divorced, I will hire an attorney. I will talk to my spouse now about how we would handle a divorce and document what we agree on.

- If I get cancer, I will lean on my medical insurance and my loved ones for emotional support. I need to make sure my insurance coverage is sufficient to handle a serious illness like this.

- If I die tomorrow, my family will need to know what to do. I need to create a final will and keep it updated and valid at all times. I also need to get life insurance, so my family will receive compensation.

We all have these fears in the backs of our minds. I found that simply writing them out calmed me down. But it also helped to come up with an action I could take immediately to deal with the problems that would result. Devising a plan for each possible scenario helped me to see that if any of those things happened—even if *all* of those things happened—I'd be okay. Of course, I would rather have nothing bad happen, but life does not work like that, and at least I have a tentative plan.

Obviously, in some cases, you can't plan ahead of time. If you looked at my "What If?" list from 2019, "global pandemic" would not be on it. But if we prepare for realistic, foreseeable probabilities, we will be in a more favorable position to handle the unexpected.

MONEY MATTERS

Musicians love to bash bar owners, saying that all they care about is money. They love to pretend they're only in music for the art of it and to express themselves.

Yet these same musicians want the best guitars, beautiful drum sets, stylish clothes, the latest sound-editing software, and state-of-the-art computers. Newsflash: all of that costs money. I'm not sayin' that you should be a slave to the mean green. But don't be hasty to act like you're too good for money when you need it just like everybody else.

And you don't need money only to make music. You need it for emergencies. You need it when the world goes up in flames. When you're young, you feel a certain sense of invincibility, but that's not reality. It's not a matter of *if* shit will happen but *when*, and trust me, it will. So I strongly urge you to plan your finances now for any eventualities. Being a slave to poverty is a lot worse.

Like so many people, a lot of musicians don't have cash on hand. They choose to live on credit—basically, borrowed money—accumulating substantial debts plus compounding interest on the unpaid balance. When monthly payments are due, most pay only the minimum, and that's when their financial downward spiral journey begins. I've been there. But once I came to my senses, I refused to ever put myself in such a predicament again.

Debt

When my future wife, Julie, and I moved to Asia in 1997, I was personally $37,000 in debt, and I was sick of it.

Rewind to a few months earlier. I needed cash to upgrade some of my equipment for our gigs in Asia. As was often the case, I called my older brother Nick, who had planned for great financial stability and who was always there for me, and asked for yet another loan. But this time, I felt a knot in my stomach. I felt shame. As I hung up the phone, I turned to Julie and said, "I will never make that call again." I had a deep need to get out of debt. I was done being broke. Financially speaking, anybody will tell you to pay your credit card debt first because you're racking up 19 percent in annual interest, which compounds on a daily basis if you don't pay it off. I actually paid my personal debt first, the money I owed my brother Nick, even though there was zero interest, because I can't sleep when I owe a friend or family member money.

At the same time I was paying personal debt, I started reading books about getting out of debt, and I began saving as much as I could. I also started paying down my credit cards. I had four at the time, so I paid the minimum on the three with the highest balance and as much as I could afford on the one with the smallest balance. Once the personal debt to Nick was paid off, I started paying a little more each month toward the card that had the lowest balance. When that one was paid off, I cut up the card and canceled the account, and started putting a little more toward the second card. If I had been paying fifty bucks a month toward the first and ten bucks toward the second, I started paying sixty toward the second once the first was paid in full.

Owning credit cards is necessary—you almost can't function in society without one—but keep in mind that you should never spend more than you earn. The problem was that for many years, I went out and charged more stuff every time I paid off a card, so I was never really out of debt. It was a weight hanging around my neck that took years to drop. Now, I've systematized credit card payments so that they are always paid in full. In some cases I actually have a credit because I pay more than the balance.

After all the debt was paid off, I would periodically call the credit bureau for fun and ask, "Can you tell me what my credit rating is please?"

The person on the other end of the line would say, "Sir, your credit rating is excellent."

"Could you say that again?"

"It's excellent, sir."

"Thanks very much."

It was music to my ears. I'm still a stupid spender to this day, but I never spend above my means.

Saving

Getting out of debt takes serious discipline. You have to want it, plan for it, systematize it. At the same time you're paying down what you owe, you have to start saving. Remember, shit will happen, and if you don't have money saved, you'll need to borrow money from someone or put those unexpected expenses on your credit card and end up back in debt.

Many financial experts say that you should save a minimum of 20 percent of your income each month and live on the other 80 percent. To get out of debt as quickly as possible, Julie and I flipped that model and we agreed to live on 10 to 15 percent of our combined incomes for about a year and put the rest toward saving and paying down debt. Of course, we were living in hotels for free during those days, and our food and laundry were also free, so that made it a lot easier to live on so little, but we still saved like crazy. We even paid our mortgage on our house in five years instead of twenty-five. Our only splurge was Sunday night dinner, because we only had one day off. We'd spend around two hundred dollars on a really nice meal with a bottle of wine. We were making what would be considered minimum wage in the music industry, but because we were disciplined and took advantage of the perks, we paid off our debts, and we never once felt like we were suffering. We were enjoying an exciting and wonderful lifestyle.

When my partner Marc and I started our company, el-live Productions, we made saving a priority and created an emergency fund. We both agreed that we could live one month without pay, so to kickstart the emergency fund, we deposited the equivalent of that amount. Then each month, we would put our well-earned money toward our emergency fund first. If we didn't have as many gigs that month and didn't have money left after paying the fund, we simply didn't get paid. Then we decided to increase our goal. We evaluated our fixed expenses and considered what would happen if we lost half our company's revenue. Could the company survive for six months? We saved enough until we were sure we could.

I went on to do the same thing with my personal finances to make sure that my family would be okay if I suddenly couldn't work anymore. Would they be able to survive six months? A year? Every year or so, I would add another year's worth to my savings. Today, we enjoy life to the fullest without blinking an eye because our finances are well in order.

You can do the same thing. The numbers are clear. You know how much you spend weekly, monthly, and yearly. Figure out how much you have to save to stay afloat for a month and then a year or three or five. Not only are you investing in your future, but you're also buying yourself precious time, peace of mind, and freedom. And do yourself a favor: automate your savings so that you never see the money; it goes straight to your account.

A few years after I started the company, one of my best musicians called me and said, "G, I need $3,000."

I said, "Oh, okay, what for?"

He said, "I need to buy a computer." First of all, he didn't *need* a computer. He was just another musician jonesing for the next shiny gadget, but I didn't tell him that. I said, "Bro, you've been with me, busting your ass and earning money for six years, and you don't have $3,000?"

"No, bro," he replied. He had way too many girlfriends for his own good, and he paid to fly some of them to whatever city or country he was performing in, but he didn't have a dime to his name to buy himself a computer.

I went back to the office and told Marc, "This is crazy. I don't ever want to see this happen to one of our musicians again." It broke my heart to decline lending him the money because he was a wonderful guy, very hardworking.

This weighed on me heavily, so I called all my musicians one by one and convinced most of them to do what Julie and I did. I explained that they could easily live on a fraction of their income. I told them, "Here's the deal. If you sign up to save, I will only give you a fraction of your pay each month. I'll save the rest for your future. Unless there is truly an emergency, you can't start calling me every month for money. If we can't have this agreement, don't sign up. Are we cool?"

Some of them managed to live quite comfortably on 10 to 15 percent of their earnings a year. I didn't let any of them take more than 30 percent; that was part of the agreement. Every month I received several reports from my office team, and the first one I read was the savings report. I was so happy to see their savings increase, and I loved watching them watch their balances grow. So many of them had never seen savings in their account. It was one of the most fulfilling things I've done, and they were beside themselves in excitement.

Then the pandemic hit, gigs dropped off, and many musicians got stuck in a different country far from home. But they were okay because they had been saving. We offered to send them most of their money, but because they were already used to living on a budget, they only wanted smaller amounts. To me, saving is like taking a picture. It doesn't mean much when you take it, but it will mean the world years down the road. Take a picture. Start by saving at least 25 percent of your income and increase over time. Trust the process.

Buying a House

I'm a big believer in buying a house. Again, that's the Lebanese in me. For as long as I can remember, my parents told my siblings and me, "Buy a house!" It was just part of our culture, a way to stay connected to family who had previously all lived in the same houses and neighborhoods their whole lives.

I've heard people say, "A house is not an investment. It's a liability." I agree, but only to a certain extent. It's true that a house costs money and is not an investment in the near term. It is also true that there are other and better ways to invest in general and that you can't spend bricks the way you can withdraw money from a bank. But a house is an emotional and psychological investment: it's *your* house. If everything else goes to shit, you still go home to *your* bed in *your* house. And once it's paid off, you become a home-owner in the real sense of the word.

Owning your own home cuts down on the dumb spending. It forces you to become more disciplined as you save because, like it or not, you have to pay that mortgage.

Owning a home can also help you become more responsible and mature. If you're renting a room from Mom and someone in the band pisses you off, it's easy to say "screw you" and quit. Mom will keep supporting you, right? If you have a mortgage, however, you won't be so hasty. You'll realize that maybe it's time to grow up and try to work things out, so you can keep your job and your home.

Some of you may be thinking, "It's not that easy, man. My credit's bad. I don't have any savings. I can't just buy my own house."

Don't let the struggle keep you from achieving the dream. If you can't buy a house right away, start small: buy a studio apartment. Then a few years later, sell it and buy a one-bedroom place. A few years after that, you could sell it and buy a two-bedroom apartment. The point is, buy something now, even if it's small, and then size up, little by little. If you can't afford to buy in downtown Sydney, Montreal, or Los Angeles, buy something an hour away from the city—anywhere. Just buy something. And if you manage to rent it out, it'll pay for itself.

Nowadays, especially in North America, buying a property is fairly simple. If you can put 10 to 20 percent down and provide proof of employment, the bank will assist with the rest. You just have to think it through and figure it out. Decide you're going to buy something, start saving, and then do it.

You have no idea how many times I've had this conversation with my musicians. I beg them to save money. Just *start* saving, so they can get a house—or an apartment or a studio. Some of them have listened, and not one of them has regretted it. Not one of them has lost their house, no matter what happened.

Start small if you need to, but start.

Investing

A good friend of mine always used to say, "Georges, 'job' stands for 'just over broke.' J-O-B." It's true: a job will not get you ahead in life, financially speaking, no matter how much a company pays you. This is where investing comes in.

When I started investing I had no idea what I was doing. So I started reading about investing three or four hours a day. I spent hours analyzing stocks. At that time, the internet was pretty rough, but I read about The Motley Fool (fool.

com) in a magazine, so I started scrolling through the website. I started investing, and I lost everything. Twice. When I say, "everything," I mean *everything*. Nevertheless, I eventually did well for myself, and now, twenty-three years later, I'd consider myself an above-average investor. When you invest money in the stock market, you're playing the long game. Again, this is about discipline. I automated my contributions and didn't focus on the quick buck. I stayed away from day trading and invested monthly in companies that I loved and understood and used their products daily. I'm certainly no professional, but I've read enough to know that day trading for the quick win is not for me.

The stock market is just one way to invest money. My brothers, for example, are amazing at real estate, especially Nick. That said, some real estate investors I know have millions in assets but don't have one dollar in cash. I know many people who own buildings, apartments, and shopping malls worth $20 million, but they don't have cash on hand for emergencies. Asset rich and money poor—don't make that mistake. You want to be able to reach into your "rainy day" fund and grab $100, $200, $500 *when*, not *if*, you need it.

If you have an extra $1,000 lying around, don't invest it right away. Or, at least, don't invest all of it. A good rule of thumb is to save 15 percent of money you would otherwise turn over to your portfolio. If you have $1,000, keep $150 in savings. If you have $10,000, $1,500 of it should be within reach. You want some cash money under the pillow. (Remember, I'm not a financial advisor. I'm just sharing what I've learned.)

The goal of any investment is financial independence, meaning you don't have to work anymore because your investments are doing so well. I know this sounds crazy, but at some point you should be making more money while you're sleeping than while you're awake—your passive income should exceed your active income. You should be able to take a day or two off when you want to without going into debt.

To do this, you have to invest intelligently. It doesn't have to be a lot of money; you just have to be consistent. Youth is your greatest ally in investing, so start early so you can take full advantage of compounding interest. If you're past youth, no worries. Just start now! It's never too late. (There are tons of books on that subject. You can start with the short list in Track 9.)

Financial independence doesn't mean you can't work, just that you don't have to if you don't want to. Every teenager's dream, right? Whatever you end up doing with your time from that point on, it's your choice. You can gig into your eighties because you want to.

Insurance

My son, Julian, suffered from stomach issues when he was very young. Every time we took him to the doctor, we would hear, "Oh, it's probably something he ate."

Then when he was twelve, the issues got worse. He stopped eating and became skinny and very ill. He had pus coming out of his mouth. His body started shutting down from the inside.

We rushed him to a hospital in Vietnam, but they didn't have the proper equipment to test him, so we immediately got on a plane and flew to a more equipped hospital in Bangkok, where we found out he had Crohn's disease. We rented an apartment and did everything we could to help him. Within six weeks, we had racked up $90,000 in medical expenses. Thank God I had insurance, but even still our out-of-pocket medical expenses were $30,000. Without insurance, we could have been ruined financially.

You really have no idea what could happen in life, so you have to be prepared. Saving is one way; getting insurance is another. Get health insurance, homeowners insurance, musical equipment insurance, travel insurance, disability insurance—get it all because shit happens. It's worth the few hundred bucks a month.

FACILITATORS

Nobody makes it on their own. We all need help. We've all borrowed money at some point, and I may have to do it again tomorrow because, say it with me, shit happens.

Nick is more to me than my eldest brother; he's more like a godfather to me and to many other members of our family. He took our family under his wing and moved us all to Canada. Nick was also a facilitator in my life, someone I could really count on to help me make my dreams come true. He loaned me money to buy my first business. He loaned me money for my first sound system and for the sampler that eventually got torched.

Having facilitators like Nick is not always about money. Sometimes, you need someone trustworthy to call when you're having a hard time and need to vent with a safe person for two minutes. Words aren't going to get you out of trouble, but sharing them with someone who loves you can remind you that you're not alone when you're facing life's challenges.

The good news is that if you follow the suggestions about building relationships, keeping in touch with people, and treating people the way you want to be treated, you likely already have a team of special people that you can rely on—and who can rely on you. From beginning to end and everything in between, this business is all about people, people, people.

YOU NEVER KNOW WHAT CAN HAPPEN

In December 2019, my company was at its peak. We had ninety-seven traveling musicians, thirty-seven of which were in China. Over the years, I had never paid much attention to SARS or the latest news sensation; ignorance is bliss, sometimes. But I started hearing that something was happening in Wuhan, a virus, and something felt different about this.

I was in China at that time, and I called up a few of my Chinese friends. "What's up, guys?" I asked. "I heard about this virus."

"No, no," they said, "don't worry about it, Georges."

"No, I heard they closed down an entire city." That's no small feat in China, where cities are 25 million people—the size of the whole country of Canada.

My friends continued to tell me not to worry about it, but something didn't feel right. I flew back to Vietnam in early January 2020, and that night I couldn't sleep. At four in the morning, I sat up in bed. I turned and woke my wife up and said, "Something is not right."

"What's wrong?"

"This virus thing. Something is not right. These are people's children under my watch. If our son was in one of those bands, what would you want the boss to do? I'm flying everyone out."

"When?"

"Today."

"You can't do that."

"I can do whatever the fuck I want."

First thing that morning, one by one, I called all the general managers of the hotels. "Bro, I'm taking the band out."

"What? Are you crazy?" they said. "You're overreacting, Georges. If you do this, I won't work with you again."

"Bro, no one is going to get hurt under my watch. It's one thing to have an accident. It's another thing to know something serious is about to happen and be complacent about it. I'm taking them out."

I called my entire office team and told them to get ready to help me with logistics. Then I called all of the bands and said, "Pack now. Everyone leaves today." They were freaking out—some of them hadn't even heard about the virus—but my guys know me and trust me: when I start talking like that, there's no going back.

Within twenty-four hours we shipped everyone out—everyone except for one musician, and we made him sign a paper stating that he did not want to leave.

Forty-eight hours later, China shut down.

In December 2019, the coronavirus hadn't made the news in Canada or America yet. My family couldn't understand me; they thought I was hysterical. I told them, "It's coming. You'll see, this one is coming."

Little did I know that we would lose 100 percent of our business in three and a half weeks. As countries shut down, the phone calls came in from all over the world canceling gigs because of the shutdowns: Korea, Thailand, Malaysia, the Philippines, Singapore, United Arab Emirates, Qatar, Oman. Some musicians got stranded in the cities where they were playing, and others got stuck in cities where their flights had layovers. We started renting apartments in Spain, Vietnam, Qatar, the Philippines, and wherever our musicians got stranded. We put them up for about three and a half months. Thank goodness we had that emergency fund in place.

Everyone has their own COVID story. This pandemic has wreaked havoc on so many lives all over the world. It's the ultimate picture of the unexpected shit that can happen overnight—and it's why you need to write a "What If?" list and start saving now. Build that team of facilitators now. Be prepared for the unexpected. Take care of those around you. This is your most important gig for life.

CHALLENGE

WRITE A "WHAT IF?" LIST

This challenge is obvious: write a "What If?" list. Don't overthink it. Write every scenario you can think of, from bad to devastating. This can be scary and morbid, I know, but just go ahead and do it.

After each possible event, write one or two actions that you can take now that will make the situation a little easier if it happens. Start a contingency plan where needed. As soon as you're done, you will feel lighthearted and happy because shit will happen, but it's okay because you know what you're doing.

Share a solution to one of your *ifs* on social media, and tag me with #shithappens #gigforlife.

TAKE A BOW

Music is magical. When your band clicks and you're all grooving so tight that you become one with your instruments, and the audience is swept up into the giant ball of joy you're creating—there is nothing like it. It's almost a religious experience that leaves you feeling like everything is right in the world.

Music has the power to make the most hardened criminal cry. It can take someone back twenty years to when they were driving down the road with a friend. It can suddenly and vividly bring to mind an evening out with a high school friend or a holiday with Mom. Music is one of the most powerful forces on the planet.

Being a musician who has the ability to create this power involves challenges that go far beyond learning notes and practicing your instrument. The goal of this book is to help you embrace these challenges, own them, and overcome them, so they don't rob you of the joy of music and cause you to give up on your dream. You can be the musician you want to be, playing part-time and full-time gigs far into your golden years—*if* you are willing to work the system, set up the structure, and treat your band like the business it is.

Remember, your art needs structure. My invitation to you is to build that structure from the beginning. Embrace the system. Own it. Become excellent at executing it. That's what will give you control of your music career and your life. That's what will make it possible to share the joy that only musicians can produce.

WORK, WORK, WORK

Some of you may still be thinking that this sounds impossible. You may be confident in your musical talent, but the rest of the business aspects may scare the shit out of you. I'm not going to lie: getting started in this business can be challenging. I know many musicians who have run into issues. As you've learned, I've certainly run into my fair share of issues over the years, and I still do to this day.

When I moved to Canada at age fourteen, I didn't speak English or French. I had never played the drums or taken a music class. All I knew was that I loved music, and I wanted to be John Travolta.

Eight years later, I was leading my own band and booking gigs nearly every night of the week.

My secret? Dedication and hard work. I worked in the family pizzeria, learned two languages, learned the drums, learned business, bought my own pizzeria, invested, failed in my investments, invested again, worked to get into university, started a band, started another band, learned sound, tried my system, failed, and tried my system again until it clicked. Along the way I married the girl of my dreams, had an amazing son, bought a house, traveled the world, and developed relationships with people that have lasted decades. I have been a professional musician for the last thirty-five years, both on and off the stage, and it was all possible because I worked hard. I put into practice the things I'm sharing in this book.

I've also seen how my different experiences and talents came together over the years to make me unique in my industry. All of my assets and skills combined to connect the necessary dots that have enabled me to enjoy a long, challenging, exhilarating, and successful career.

The same is true for you. Look at what you already know as a musician or songwriter or producer or graphic designer. Connect the dots and see how all of your experiences and skills give you something unique to offer as a band leader. As a musician, you know that you play an instrument by moving one finger after another. When you play them together, you have a chord. Working this system is no different. It's rudiments. It's a paradiddle, a melody, a chord, a song. You know how to work in progression like this, one step at a time. Apply the same technique to your music career, and you'll have a gig for life.

KNOW WHEN TO TAKE A BOW

Even if you build a successful career and play well into your golden years, there comes a time when you have to say goodbye. Even the great Michael Jordan had to retire.

As a musician or band, the time to move on might come when the gig becomes stale, or when you get stuck in a certain style that became unpopular a long, long time ago, or when you no longer look forward to the gig. If any of these happen, don't continue playing just because you don't know what else to do. That's not good for anyone—you, your bandmates, or your audience.

Having a gig for life means you get to decide when it's time to move on, perhaps to another type of gig. Playing Top 40 may no longer suit you, and jumping up and down while screaming may not work at fifty-five or sixty, but you can start playing gigs that suit you, like laid-back trio or some blues.

Whatever you do, don't hang on. Know when to take a bow. If you don't, someone else might make the decision for you, and that never feels good.

THE PROJECT OF YOU

I do hope you use this book to launch your music career, but even more, I hope you use it to improve your life as a whole, to become a better you. That's what happened to me during my drum lessons with Chuck when I was a teenager. Yes, I learned music, but even more importantly, I started the biggest project of my life: improving myself.

The project of you is what makes life worth living each day. It's a never-ending journey that will ultimately make you a better husband or wife, son or daughter, friend, bandmate, partner to bar owners, and fans. Remember where we started this book: me. That project never ends because the biggest room in the world is the room for improvement.

So let's think about the project of you. Where do you want to be in twenty years? Ten years? Three years? Right now, write down a list of professional and personal goals that you want to achieve, like these for example:

- I want to start a band.
- I want to get my first gig.
- I want to play music all over the world.

- I want to finish writing my album.
- I want to lose twenty pounds.
- I want to jog three miles a day.
- I want to spend more time with my mom.
- I want to have a studio.
- I want to get married and have kids.
- I want to write a book.
- I want to start a business.

From that list, chose two things—one personal and one professional—to work on for the next twelve weeks. For example, if you want to climb Mount Everest someday, what can you do in the next twelve weeks to get started? You can watch a few videos about others who have done it, buy gear, and so on. Then break that down even more: what can you do this month? This week? Today? And then get to work!

Remember our lesson from Track 2: one pizza at a time. Some of these tasks may seem huge and impossible. Just keep asking yourself what's next. Don't give up on your dreams, personal or professional, just because they're hard to reach. Everyone faces fears and difficulties. Those who love music more than they hate the work will succeed. Think about all the positivity that reaching your goal will bring to your life, and go for it.

All of my life's failures are embedded in my successes, so I don't see them as failures anymore. They're just part of my journey.

My hope is that you do the same. Work the system. Work on yourself. Respect your partners and focus on their goals as well as yours. Treat every gig like it's Saturday night, and you'll enjoy a long, fruitful, and satisfying career doing what you love.

ACKNOWLEDGMENTS

To my ultimate band—my family, friends, band members, bar owners, audience, and support teams around the world. You have enriched my life, and I am forever grateful. I love you. G.

Special thanks to the wonderful Gail Fay, who played the role of producer throughout the writing of this book. She was always there to say "more of this and less of that" as I had my ups and downs along the way.

Also, a great big thank-you to Libby Allen and the entire team at Scribe Media. You guys rock.

ABOUT THE AUTHOR

Georges Elchakieh is the founder and CEO of el-live Productions, a highly trusted live bands production house in Asia and the Middle East. He started his music career as a drummer and formed his first band at age twenty-three while studying music at Concordia University in Montreal. Ten years later, Georges was gigging all over the world. In his thirty-five years as a professional musician, Georges has worked at every level of the business as a drummer, front man, band leader, bar owner, and show producer and trained hundreds of musicians who performed all over the world. Georges is passionate about sharing his life's ambitions, successes, wisdom, and many lessons learned, at times, with tough love.

Milton Keynes UK
Ingram Content Group UK Ltd.
UKHW041810010823
426115UK00027B/466/J